# TINY'S STORIES

## AN ATHABASCAN FAMILY ON THE YUKON RIVER

*by*
*Theresa "Tiny" Nellie Demientieff Devlin*
*with Sam Demientieff*

## CIRQUE PRESS

*Tiny's Stories*
Copyright © 2023 Jack Devlin

All rights reserved. No part of this publication may be reproduced, distributed or transmitted in any form or by any means, including photocopying, recording, or other electronic or mechanical methods, without the prior written permission of the publisher, except in the case of brief quotations embodied in critical reviews and certain other noncommercial uses permitted by copyright law.

*Published by*

Sandra Kleven — Michael Burwell
3157 Bettles Bay Loop
Anchorage, AK 99515

cirquejournal@gmail.com | cirquejournal.com

*Photos* are from the Devlin and Demientieff family collections, except as otherwise noted.
*Cover and text design* by Moontide Design
*Production assistance* by Snowshoeword

First Edition September 2023

ISBN: 979-8-89342-641-0

## TINY DEVLIN
August 18, 1945–February 4, 2020

*This book is dedicated to the memory of Tiny's son,
Justin Nicholas Sisson Devlin
May 11, 1969–October 3, 2004*

# CONTENTS

FOREWORD By Carroll Hodge .................................................................. 8

INTRODUCTION—*SOME HISTORICAL PERSPECTIVE* by Samuel S. Demientieff ................................. 11

OUR DEMIENTIEFF FAMILY ................................................................. 16
    NICK E. DEMIENTIEFF, DAD .......................................................... 17
    NELLIE MAE BRESSLER, MOM ....................................................... 18
    THEIR MARRIAGE ....................................................................... 20
    CHILDREN ................................................................................. 21
    MY BEGINNINGS–AUGUST 18, 1945 ................................................ 24

LIFE IN HOLY CROSS ...................................................................... 25
    The VILLAGE ............................................................................ 25
    OUR HOUSE ............................................................................. 27
    SUNDAYS .................................................................................. 28
    SUNDAYS after CHURCH ............................................................. 29
    FISH HEARTS and AUNTIE TATIANA ............................................ 30
    FISH CAMP ............................................................................... 32
    EASTER DRESS ......................................................................... 33
    The DUNKING .......................................................................... 35
    RAINY DAYS and BLIND JACK .................................................... 36
    GOING for WATER .................................................................... 36
    CANDY from the STORE ............................................................ 37
    EVENING GHOSTS .................................................................... 38
    MORE EVENING GHOSTS .......................................................... 39
    MRS. ANTHONY and the BEARS ................................................. 39
    MOM and DAD'S ANNIVERSARY ................................................ 40
    PARTNERS ................................................................................ 41

LIFE ON THE RIVER ........................................................................ 43
    *OUR BOATS* by Sam Demientieff .................................................. 43

*MAPS* ........................................................................................ 48–51
    RIVER ADVENTURES .................................................................. 52
    The PILOTHOUSE of the *SEA WOLF* ............................................ 53
    The PADDLEWHEEL ................................................................... 54
    The *BEAVER* ............................................................................ 56
    The BEAR on the *BEAVER* .......................................................... 57
    BIRDIE'S a BOY ........................................................................ 59
    IRENE the BAKER ..................................................................... 60
    The STOLEN BIRTHDAY ............................................................. 60
    PLAY TIME ............................................................................... 62
    TIME OFF ................................................................................ 63
    TRAVELING the INNOKO RIVER to FLAT .................................... 65
    TOOTSIE CROSBIE .................................................................... 67
    The FLAT SALOON ................................................................... 68

LIFE IN FAIRBANKS ........................................................................ 70
    FAIRBANKS and CHANGE .......................................................... 71
    SCHOOL .................................................................................. 73

| | |
|---|---|
| The CITY | *74* |
| OUR NEIGHBORHOOD GROCERY STORE | *76* |
| BEING SICK | *77* |
| WINTER FUN | *78* |
| INDOOR FUN | *80* |
| NEW HOLIDAYS | *82* |
| MOM'S WAY | *84* |
| "WHEN CROWS TURN WHITE" | *86* |
| MOM, the CREATURE WHISPERER | *87* |
| **BACK ON THE RIVER: FAIRBANKS TO HOLY CROSS** | *88* |
| RIVER REFLECTIONS | *89* |
| NENANA | *91* |
| "THE RIVER OPENS WIDE" | *92* |
| **HOLY CROSS MISSION SCHOOL, 1952** | *95* |
| BOARDING at HOLY CROSS MISSION | *96* |
| The MISSION BUILDINGS | *97* |
| The SISTERS of SAINT ANN | *97* |
| BOARDING SCHOOL LIFE | *98* |
| CHORES | *100* |
| SUNDAYS at the MISSION | *101* |
| PICNIC in the MEADOW | *102* |
| SISTER MARY ALICE and the MUCKINJACKS | *103* |
| The MOVIE HALL | *104* |
| LONESOME DAYS | *105* |
| FIRST FLIGHT | *106* |
| **COPPER VALLEY SCHOOL, 1958 to 1964** | *108* |
| The BEGINNINGS of CVS | *109* |
| MY FIRST YEAR at COPPER, 7th GRADE | *109* |
| The CLASSROOM | *110* |
| DANCE INSTRUCTION | *112* |
| The BANQUET | *113* |
| WEEKENDS | *114* |
| SMIDA—SISTER MARY IDA | *116* |
| The PANTRY | *117* |
| The FATHERS' DINING ROOM | *119* |
| BASKETBALL | *119* |
| DECEMBER | *121* |
| A DEATH in the FAMILY | *122* |
| MY SECOND YEAR at COPPER, 8th GRADE | *125* |
| SISTER MARY ALICE | *125* |
| MORNINGS | *126* |
| CVS GLEE CLUB, 1960 to 1961 | *128* |
| The SPIRIT of COPPER VALLEY | *130* |
| **TINY'S EPILOGUE** | *132* |
| **MEMORIAL BIOGRAPHY of THERESA "TINY" DEVLIN**  *by Jack Devlin and Sam Demientieff* | *134* |
| **ACKNOWLEDGMENTS** | *138* |

# FOREWORD

*By Carroll Hodge*

This remarkable book emerges out of Tiny (Demientieff) Devlin's memories of her childhood experiences with her Athabascan family in the Lower Yukon River region of Alaska from 1945 to 1964. Growing up as the eighth child of ten, given the nickname "Tiny" because of her small size, she developed into a determined young woman with a strong spirit and a sense of both curiosity and adventure.

The stories and memories in this book reflect Tiny's unique childhood in river villages, fish camps, mission boarding schools, and, for a time, a city school in Fairbanks. Summers were spent on the family's paddlewheel boat and barges, freighting supplies to villages along the Yukon River and visiting family and friends. Winters found the Demientieff family either in the village of Holy Cross or a log cabin outside Fairbanks. Tiny's teenage school years were spent at Copper Valley School, a Catholic boarding school near Glennallen. Wherever Tiny was, adventure and mischief seemed to follow. Fortunately for those who heard her stories and those who will read them here, she became a gifted storyteller.

In 2018, Tiny began writing her stories down, intent on turning them into a book. She asked me, a friend and former colleague, to give them a first edit. The first story she sent me would become part of "Life on the River." It introduced her ever-present curiosity and skill as an observer, as well as her early appreciation of the rhythms of her natural environment:

> One day I decided to climb up on top of the pilothouse. I climbed the ladder to the second level, walked past Mom and Dad's cabin and Lolly's cabin, then up the next ladder to the third level. It had never crossed my mind

before how high up that was… I carefully crawled along until I reached the front of the pilothouse roof. The view was amazing. I could see far in front of the barge, the flag waving, the river current and the eddies swirling about.

As 2018 moved into 2019, Tiny was spending many months in and out of the hospital with a developing lung disease. While recuperating, she continued to write of her childhood experiences in the village of Holy Cross and her connection with important traditions like harvesting fish and sharing with Elders. Her remarkable memory allowed her to retrieve these moments in detail, and write them with humor and affection.

The more stories Tiny wrote, the more she was aware of other ideas that she wanted to explore, questions she was still pondering, as she told me in this note as we were working on the book:

> Now, writing as an adult, and after having a life rich with experiences, I am revisiting my childhood, becoming aware of moments where I had questioning thoughts that I didn't understand. My experiences also gave me some answers. Sometimes they were in Dad's stories that reflected the teachings of Christ, or in how Mom lived her faith. As I learned more about the Athabascan people and their Traditional ceremonies as ways of teaching and passing on culture, I learned ways of Love, Caring and Sharing.

It seems fitting that Tiny's final story in this book, "A Near-Death Experience," is of a childhood experience of nearly drowning, and how it offered her an understanding of death: "…the transition to love, and the light."

Tiny was working on this book of her childhood and school days stories up until the time of her death in February 2020. She had plans to write about her adulthood, which would have been another abundant source of stories. She had a full life in partnership with her husband Jack Devlin, as well as being a mother, sister, daughter, auntie and friend to many. Her professional work throughout Alaska and on national advisory boards centered on nurturing community health with AIDS prevention and suicide prevention programs. Her interest in cultural revitalization led her to international travel and cultural exchanges with indigenous peoples in Australia, Brazil and Greenland. Sadly, Tiny was not able to write these later chapters of her life. However, they will be remembered by those who worked by her side, traveled with her, laughed often, and loved the good work they did together. After Tiny's death, this book was completed by family and friends. Many people helped make this publication possible. It is now a tribute to the adventuresome, courageous and much-loved person that Tiny was.

Gabriola Island, British Columbia, 2021

*Jack and Tiny, grandson Devin, daughter Jacklynn.*

# INTRODUCTION—
# SOME HISTORICAL PERSPECTIVE

*By Samuel S. Demientieff*

*I believe my sister Tiny's goal in writing her memories was to tell about her life, her experiences, and her pride in her Dine'/Athabascan heritage.*

*The span of time Tiny writes about is from 1945 to 1964, and covers her childhood years through high school. Her stories are a vivid picture of our family of twelve, the summers we spent on a paddlewheel boat and barge, carrying freight to villages along the Yukon River in Alaska, and the winters we spent in the village of Holy Cross. During these years, our family experienced the old ways as well as the new, eventually moving from village life to city life in Fairbanks, but never losing connection with our traditions.*

*Our Demientieff family is of Athabascan, Yupik, Russian, and German descent. Our Deg Xitan Athabascan ancestors are specifically the Dine' of the villages in the area of Anvik, Shageluk, Grayling and Holy Cross. The Dine' have lived along the lower Yukon River for many centuries. We received our Dine' heritage from our grandmothers, our Russian and German heritage from our grandfathers.*

*Our first known Russian ancestor is our great-grandfather, Nikolai Demten'ev, who worked at the Kolmakovski Redoubt outpost on the Kuskokwim River. It was around 1867, about the time that the United States purchased the territory of Alaska from Russia. Nikolai and his Kuskokwim Yupik wife, Pelagia, had seven children that we know of. Around 1892, four of his teenage children, Ephrem, Ivan, and two others, travelled by dogsled to the village of Holy Cross where a Catholic Mission was being constructed. The oldest son, Ephrem, was our grandfather. Over the years, he and others in the Demten'ev family contributed their hunting, fishing, riverboating and building skills to the Mission.*

*Nikolai and Pelagia with children L-R Tatiana, Petruska, Elisaveta (Elizabeth), and Aniska. Not in photo: Ephrem, Ivan, and Nick.*

*Adult children of Nikolai and Pelagia, Holy Cross, early 1890s. L-R Petruska (1879), Nicholas (1875), Aniska (1873), Tatiana (1881), Ivan (1871), Ephrem (1863). Not in photo: Elizabeth. Ephrem was Tiny's grandfather.*

*Throughout Alaska, various churches were setting up missions and schools in villages, taking in orphaned children whose parents may have died in a series of epidemics that swept through Alaska. Men were recruited from all over to help with the building of missions throughout the Kuskokwim/Yukon region.*

*The Gold Rush of 1898, in Nome and the Klondike, brought many outside people into the Yukon River country. In the 1930's, our parents invested in a boat and barge, starting a freight hauling business on the Yukon and Iditarod Rivers. In those years we brought cargo to many communities, including bringing supplies to the gold miners at Flat.*

*During World War II, the military built an airfield in Galena and housing for troops in Nenana, which increased the need for materials that could be brought in by barge. In 1945, when the war was winding down, our Demten'ev (over time, changed to Demientieff) family was living in Nenana where Tiny was born. Alaska would go through many more changes during Tiny's lifetime, but her stories reflect a time of some continuity, a childhood spent within a warm and protective family that encouraged her adventures.*

# TINY'S STORIES

# OUR DEMIENTIEFF FAMILY

*Ephrem and Agnes Demientieff family. Back L-R William, Justina, Nicholas, Mary (Alphonse's wife), and Alphonse. Seated is Agnes (holding Mary and Alphonse's child, George), and Ephrem.*

# NICK E. DEMIENTIEFF, DAD

My Dad was born into a family of two boys and one girl. He was strong and willful, and had a streak of humor and mischief. When he was in the second grade, he ran away from school and his parents must have realized that this independent young boy made up his mind starting at a very early age.

Perhaps because he didn't go to school, he didn't hear negative comments that would erode his spirit. He generally listened to what others had to say—this helped him form his own opinions—rather than seeking the approval of an outside authority. He learned how to read, write and do math, and he always had a current copy of the *Alaska Magazine* on hand.

*Nicholas Ephrem Demientieff*

Although he had missed out on a Western-style education, he had spent his boyhood learning the traditional skills of hunting and fishing. Setting snares and running a trap line kept him busy helping to provide for his aging parents.

# NELLIE MAE BRESSLER, MOM

Mom was the older of two sisters, the daughter of a German father, Samuel Bressler, and an Athabascan mother, Cora Young. Her parents had two daughters, Nellie and Jessie. Nellie's mom passed away, leaving her dad with the two little girls.

As a fur trapper, her dad moved around a lot, and when he realized he couldn't take care of his daughters, he placed them in the Episcopal Mission in the village of Anvik, upriver from Holy Cross.

Mom was not a traditional Native girl, because she reflected the Episcopal teachers she had in Anvik. She grew into a nice-looking young woman, gentle and a little shy. No child was too small, too shy or any less important than another to my mom. She connected at a level that didn't need words—her actions were more powerful.

*Nellie with first child, Eva, born in 1931.*

*Nick and Nellie with Eva.*

*At the trapping cabin. Nellie (holding second child, Floyd), Nick, Eva.*

*Wedding photo, April 21, 1929. At Holy Cross church, after the double wedding of Alfred and Marianne Gurtler, Nick and Nellie Demientieff.*

# THEIR MARRIAGE

Dad grew into a handsome young man with a strong stature and great determination. Getting word there was a good-looking young woman named Nellie Mae Bressler in the Anvik Mission, Dad had to go and see for himself. Sure enough, he fell in love with Nellie, who had grown up to be quite striking.

Nellie was raised in the Episcopal Mission while Dad was raised as a Catholic. This difference didn't cross Dad's mind when he and Nellie went to the priest in Holy Cross and asked him to marry them. The priest questioned Nellie's faith, since she was not a member of the Catholic Church. He told Dad that the marriage just couldn't happen. Dad responded, "If you don't marry us, then we'll go to Flat and have the justice of the peace do it."

The Holy Cross priest quickly changed his mind and, on April 21, 1929, there was a double wedding for Dad and Mom with our Auntie Marianne and Uncle Alfred Gurtler.

*Nick and Nellie Demientieff at their 50th wedding celebration, 1979.*

# CHILDREN

Mom and Dad had ten children, three boys and seven girls, each born two years apart. I was number eight, so the older kids were already grown up when I came along.

Eva was the first born, in 1931. Manny (Floyd Joseph) was the first son. Later on, when we were on the river and Manny was learning the ropes of becoming a riverboat captain, he was usually in the pilothouse, giving Dad breaks and time to relax. Lolly (Caroline Justina), was child number three. She had the same spirit as Dad and he entrusted her with the responsibilities of family photographer. She was also in charge of inventory for each river trip. She was a second mom for us younger kids.

Bing (Nicholas Ephrem) was the second son—quieter, but definitely mischievous. He helped out as a deck hand and he and Birdie never ran short of friends in all of the villages. Birdie (Samuel Sergi) was the youngest of the boys, with curly brown hair, brown eyes and a winning smile. Lumpy (Joanne Helen) came next; she looked a lot like Mom, and was popular among the many cousins. Irene (Irene Agnes) was quiet and quite serious. She kept a close eye on the three of us youngest kids, which took up much of her time.

Then there's me, Tiny (named Nellie, later Theresa). When Mom laid eyes on me, she called me "Tiny," probably because I was the smallest of her babies. Mom kept a vigilant eye on me but let me be the wild, mischievous, strong-willed child.

Sugar (Shirley Frances) was two years younger than me, but taller, so sometimes treated me like her younger sister. Tootie (Rita Delores) was the baby, and the only one with blond hair and blue eyes. I don't think she knew how to get mad or hold a grudge; she was too busy enjoying life.

As our family grew, Dad and Mom kept us all together as a family, even on the boats as they continued freighting supplies every summer along the Yukon River.

*Steamboats and barges at Nenana shipyard.*

*Photo of the Demientieff family in about 1953. Almost all of the siblings had nicknames that all family members used for them throughout their childhoods and beyond. In* Tiny's Stories, *names or nicknames are used as Tiny originally wrote them, without explanation. Here's a "key" for readers:*

Back row L-Rt:
    Irene
    Sam – "Birdie"
    Carolyn – "Lolly"
    Nick, Jr. – "Bing"
    Joanne – "Lumpy"

Middle row L-R:
    Eva
    Nellie
    Nick
    Floyd – "Manny"

Front row L-R:
    Nellie Theresa – "Tiny"
    Rita – "Tootie"
    Shirley – "Sugar"

# MY BEGINNINGS—
# AUGUST 18, 1945

The night I was born, there was a flood in Nenana and Dad and the older boys were away working on the boat. The rest of our family was asleep in our house, a former military house that was in a line of Army houses and tents. Doctors and nurses lived nearby in a building with a red cross on the door. During the night, Mom woke my older sister Lolly and told her to get the Army doctor—and not to come back without him. "Keep knocking until he answers that door!"

So Lolly went to the house with the red cross on the door and banged on it until the doctor answered. She brought him back to the house, showed him Mom's bedroom, and went to bed. When Lolly woke up, there was no noise in the house but Mom had a new baby with her in bed. Lolly asked her where she'd gotten this baby, asked her was that why the doctor had come, and how come the new baby didn't make a sound. When Lolly asked what her name was, Mom told her, "She's just… tiny," and it became my nickname.

# LIFE IN HOLY CROSS

## The VILLAGE

The village of Holy Cross is located on the lower Yukon River, which flows south from the Interior of Alaska and west to the Bering Sea. The people are primarily Athabascan (Dine') Indian, although the village is located on a border of sorts: it's the last village on the river in Athabascan territory and is at the beginning of Yupik Eskimo territory.

*Holy Cross from the south, looking upriver. In the left foreground, people are working on mission potato fields and gardens.*

During my childhood, there was a sprawling meadow and hills with spruce and birch trees surrounding the community. The largest hill stood over the village like a crown, with a large white cross and a perfect vantage point that looked over the village and the mighty Yukon River. The surrounding hills framed the village and the Holy Cross Catholic Mission, the gardens and the sawmill. The mission was located above the village and was a huge compound of buildings. Although the Mission and the village shared a close setting, each was quite separate; their only connection was the church.

*Holy Cross. Nick in front of Demientieff family house built by his father, Ephrem. Skilled river man Ivan "Cap" Demientieff and his brother Ephrem were also lumber millers and carpenters. Their sawmill produced dimensional lumber and joinery products. By the early 20th century, finely built frame buildings were replacing early log structures at Holy Cross. In this photo Nick is hauling firewood with a special articulating snogo sled he designed and built (information from Sam Demientieff).*

# OUR HOUSE

Our house gave us a view of the dirt road that connected the village to the Mission and the meadow. We could see the tops of the other houses, the slough, the little steam bath houses and the lower end of the village. The kitchen had a huge wood stove and was at the back of the house.

Off the kitchen area was Mom and Dad's bedroom, and a staircase led up to the second floor that was one big room of beds. For the younger kids, Mom made these huge pillows filled with feathers that were our mattresses. I remember how soft and warm they were at night. The rest of the beds were for the older kids and were like military metal beds with regular mattresses.

*The Holy Cross mission building, laundry, church, Jesuit House to left, with a vegetable garden in foreground. Note the Russian architectural influence in the church building.*

## SUNDAYS

Sundays always started off with all of us fussing around getting ready to attend Mass. The single bell of the church rang a slow and steady call to us, as if saying, "Time to get ready," and Mom would hurry us up. There was a second bell that would announce when Mass was about to start.

Our family would make our way up the dirt road between the huge gardens to the church. My grandpa and his brothers helped build the church, and their Russian ancestry helped influence the Russian style architecture. It was a very beautiful church. The front faced the Yukon River and was painted white with green trim on the windows and doors. Someone planted two rows of birch trees that fringed a pathway from the church to the riverbank.

Inside, on each side of the entrance, there were holy water fonts—places to dip our fingers into the water and be blessed while entering. In those early days of the church, the altar faced away from the congregation. Above the altar there was a large cross with the body of Jesus nailed to the cross. There were a number of statues, and large chairs stood at the front for the priest and the altar boys. All this area was separated from the congregation by a communion railing.

The front right-side rows were set aside for the little Mission girls, then the bigger girls, the Sisters, and lastly, the women and children of the village. The front left side was for the younger Mission boys, then the older Mission boys, then the village boys and men. The little Mission girls all wore red and black pleated skirts, white blouses with a sash, white socks, shoes and little red and black hats—a Scottish sort of uniform. I always wanted a uniform but never did get one.

During Mass the opening prayers were all in Latin, which I didn't understand, but they sounded quite serious, quiet, and holy, so I just followed along. There were songs in Latin that were quite beautiful, melodious and holy, always ending in a long "Amen." It was all very formal and quiet—the prayers, the burning of incense, the ringing of little bells.

When the Mass concluded, the priest walked outside quietly, accompanied by a procession of holy-looking little boys wearing their black robes and white sort-of-blousy shirts. Then from both sides of the front of the church the little Mission girls and boys followed, then the older Mission children and then, finally, the village people. It was now official: Mass was over and Sunday had just gotten underway.

# SUNDAYS after CHURCH

Once we cleared out of the church, we were free to run back to the village and home. Sundays were special, as Dad usually made a nice fire and sourdough pancakes on the stovetop. Mom was free to sit and enjoy her coffee at our dining table, which was covered in a red and white oilcloth. Usually Mom's best buddy, Edna, would come over to have coffee with Mom.

After Sunday breakfast, I don't know where my older brothers and sisters disappeared off to, but Sugar, Tootie and I would head out the front door to freedom. We played marbles with our friends on the smooth ground, with a circle drawn in the mud. By the end of the game, we each walked away with a little bag containing our precious winnings. We would also gather to play games out at the sandbar, which was a huge clearing of sand and mud. We organized ourselves into teams to play Flag, Red Rover, and tag. Sometimes we waded or swam in the Yukon River, roamed the village or played in the meadow. Looking back, life then seemed so much simpler.

# FISH HEARTS and AUNTIE TATIANA

My Great-Auntie Tatiana lived up on the hill in Holy Cross. Her little house was located on a corner of the mission gardens. It had two adjoining rooms. There were two tall windows that looked out over the gardens, the village, and a beautiful view of the Yukon River. She had a little kitchen with a small dining table covered with a red and white gingham tablecloth. Her home felt warm, cozy, and welcoming—and it was always clean and cheerful.

Auntie was a kindly woman, single with no children, just herself. She played the organ for church services and she was close to the Sisters. She was quite unusual, as she was always dressed in fine clothes. My sister Lolly said, "She was a lady in waiting." I didn't understand what she was waiting for!

When the King salmon were in season, Mom and Dad, like everyone else, were busy with fishing. That included setting out fishnets, checking the nets, pulling the huge Kings loose from the nets, placing them in tubs, bringing them back to the village for cutting, cleaning, and hanging. The fish were cut into salmon strips, as well as salted for storage and our later use. We also ate a lot of fresh salmon. The work didn't ease up until the salmon run was over.

I was too small to cut fish, but I still had chores to do. I checked on the slow burning fire that sent a steady smoldering flow of smoke up to flavor the strips. Mom and Dad had a tall smokehouse, with tiers and tiers of strips. The Yukon King salmon are so rich with oil that it was tricky to run into the smoke house, check the fire, and get back out while trying to avoid the dripping oil. I helped with packing wood into the smoke house and I gathered goose grass for the smudge pot. The smudge pot helped control the mosquitoes and keep them away from Mom and Dad while they were taking care of the salmon.

It seemed like every other day I asked Mom to save the fish

hearts for me. She would collect them and call me to her worktable. She saved a nice stack of hearts. I would get a bowl from the kitchen, collect the hearts and walk up the hill to Auntie Tatiana's. She could see me coming.

*Tatiana Demientieff, sister of Tiny's grandfather, Ephrem, was the only sibling of her generation not to marry and have children. She was very important to the Holy Cross Mission:*

> *"Gifted in music and needlework, she learned to play the organ, sewed for the sisters and girls, and taught catechism and other classes. Her record of thirty-one years of volunteer service has never been surpassed" (from* **North to Share: The Sisters of Saint Ann in Alaska and the Yukon Territory,** *p. 68)*

I think I was a welcome sight. I'd climb onto a chair by the table and make myself comfortable. Auntie got busy from the moment I arrived. She'd pull out her frying pan and start cooking. Meanwhile, I would gaze out over the village and notice that she had a perfect spot to watch Mom and Dad working at their fish table. From the moment I set foot in the house, she was talking. She talked while cooking, while I ate, and, I think, while I was walking out the door. She loved to talk. Thinking back, I'm glad she didn't ask any questions. I loved Auntie Tatiana for her gentle ways and kindness.

# FISH CAMP

During the summer months when the fish were running—King salmon, Chum, Dog salmon and others—village people went to their fish camps for the season. There, everyone was occupied with checking fishnets, cleaning and cutting fish, smoking fish strips or just enjoying a meal of fresh salmon straight out of the river.

One time Dad and Mom took our boat downriver to our fish camp below Holy Cross. Dad had offered the camp to one of our Aunties because her husband had died and she had five children, so he thought it was the right thing to do. Of course, Sugar, Tootie and I had to go along with him. As we pulled the boat up to the gravel beach at the camp and tied it up, the camp was bustling with activities. There was a freshwater creek close by, and a smokehouse, fish racks, outhouse, and tented structures with wood frames for cooking and sleeping.

Auntie Frances was there with her hair pulled back and tucked into a roll, wearing an apron and glasses. She was glad to see Mom and Dad, and as they visited, I explored the camp with Sugar and Tootie. We came upon a smiling young man who invited us into one of the tents where he had a phonograph that he could wind up to play records. One of the songs, "Sixteen Tons," was sung by Tennessee Ernie Ford. His voice was deep, clear, and magical, and it stirred up my imagination.

Holy Cross was usually quieter in the summer because those who moved to fish camp took their whole families and often their dogs with them. We stayed in the village at times if our family was between boat trips, or if Mom chose to stay behind while Dad and the crew made a quick trip on the river. With most of the kids away at fish camp, Sugar, Tootie, and I did the best we could to occupy our time.

Our visit to the fish camp must have awakened my imagination to make toys to play "Fish Camp" at home. There was a way to make a makeshift Indian knife for cutting fish. I would get a lid from a vegetable can from Mom, and after cleaning it, I bent the lid in half and flattened it.

With my knife ready, I would walk among the willow bushes and cut four matched sticks, each with a Y-shaped fork in it, for the four corners of my fish drying rack. Then I would cut more willow branches, strip away their leaves and fashion them into poles for the top rack, fastening it to the four corners that would support it.

Next, I would search the willow bushes and gather the biggest leaves. These represented my "catch" of King salmon fish—and then I would gather the most slender leaves, which were my Silver salmon. I cut the leaves carefully and hung them carefully. It took quite a while, but I enjoyed it. Amazing what kids can learn just from watching their parents.

# EASTER DRESS

Everyday life was guided by the seasons. Springtime brought melting snow, warmer weather and more time spent out of doors. One spring, as Easter approached, I remember big packages that came in the mail. Mom had ordered new dresses for us and she was excited to open the boxes. The dresses were in colors of light pink, pale yellow, and mint green, and were made with very fine, thin material. You could see through the first layer and beneath was a thicker, soft material. Each dress had a sash that could tie into a nice bow in the back. We each had our own beautiful new dress.

When Easter morning arrived, Sugar, Tootie, and I decided to make our way to church, for some reason along a trail down by the riverbank. Mom was okay with this, so we started along the path and I noticed the dodowacks (old rosehip seed pods) were still on the thorn bushes. The village kids used to pick a pod, break open the top, remove the seeds and use the empty pod as a bowl for a homemade pipe. I was impressed with these older kids and I had decided to try it myself.

After I got my empty seed pod, I found a thick, hollow, dried out grass stem and fashioned it into a pipe stem. For tobacco, I used crushed, dried leaves. I thought I was so clever when I finally had the pipe together. I had remembered to bring a wooden match to light the "tobacco" leaves, and I tried to actually smoke my pipe.

*Holy Cross gathering in front of Demientieff house. In back row L-R Tiny, Irene, Nellie, others. In front L-R Tootie and Sugar, others. The family was probably getting ready for the trip back to Fairbanks (Sam Demientieff).*

As soon as the leaves started to burn, out popped an ember and it dropped onto my new nylon and silk dress, which started to melt. I managed to get the smoldering under control, but the damage was done! There were several spots on my dress that were evidence, so, in horror, I decided to go back home and change into one of my everyday cotton dresses, sure that Mom wouldn't notice.

After changing, I had to run up to the church to join the rest for Easter Mass. After the service it was Irene who noticed I was wearing my cotton dress, not the beautiful new Easter dress. She pulled me aside and asked me what happened. I told her that I didn't like the new dress, so I had changed. She didn't buy that for a minute and demanded that I show her what had happened. I dutifully led her to my hiding place and revealed the damaged dress. I don't recall what happened after that, as I seem to forget the consequences for all the times I got myself into trouble. I do not remember ever getting spanked by Mom or Dad.

# The DUNKING

All of the houses in the village had a rain barrel, usually standing at one corner of the house for a family's water supply. One rainy day, a couple of us kids were bored and up to no good. There was nothing to do and no hope of a break in the weather.

We prowled along the road and came upon one of the younger girls. She was so little—easy pickins! We hatched a plan to dunk her in a rain barrel and went straight for her. She had no chance when we picked her up and dunked her. The poor little thing came up drenched and we felt bad as she looked at us so innocently. We had at least pulled her up and out of the barrel, but that was another time when I felt the temptation to do mischief well up within me and acted on it. I wonder why such thoughts happen.

# RAINY DAYS and BLIND JACK

On rainy days the village was quieter, most work activities were shut down, and most kids were nowhere to be seen. I liked to look out the window on the second floor of our house where it faced to the south. From that vantage point I could see over the rooftops of the village, the main road connecting the village to the meadow and the lake. I watched as the rain formed a series of big puddles on the road, and I noticed how grey the sky was with thick dark clouds.

One of the older men of the village, Blind Jack, was walking along the road, using his cane. The rain didn't slow Blind Jack; he always walked freely throughout the village.

I watched as he tapped his way up the road and came closer and closer to our house. I had a flashing thought: I'll show him the way. I quickly got my jacket on and slipped into my rubber boots. I dashed out the door and then slowed myself, to calm myself down. It was not unusual to offer assistance to Jack; all one had to do was to call out his name and take the end of his cane to lead him along.

So, I took hold of his cane and started to march straight ahead towards a large puddle! As I got closer, I could feel the guilt and shame building up within me. Just before we got to the puddle, I changed my mind and managed to get him safely around a whole series of puddles. I felt the guilt melt away to relief and was actually proud of myself in the end.

# GOING for WATER

We didn't have running water in the house, so we had to go to the village well house to fetch water. This involved pulling a cart carrying five-gallon buckets. The chore was usually carried out by one of the older kids, but Sugar, Tootie and

I generally went along to the well house.

One time, Birdie drove Dad's truck to get the water and, since this was unusual and exciting, us kids had to tag along. When the filled buckets of water were loaded in the back of the truck, Birdie got ready to drive home.

Getting to sit in the front always triggered an argument among us but this time I managed to be the one to sit in the passenger seat. It wasn't often that we got to sit inside the truck instead of in the back, so I didn't know how to close the door properly. When the truck lurched forward and turned left, I was leaning on the door and it swung open somehow. I clung onto to the window and swung out over the ground. Just as quickly, the door swung back, hard enough to close it properly. It all happened so fast. I don't recall sitting up front any more.

# CANDY from the STORE

As I grew older, and perhaps more responsible, Mom entrusted me to run to the store to buy something that she needed like sugar or flour. There was only one general store in the village at the time and it belonged to George Turner, an older man who was kind to us kids.

His big store was filled with all sorts of things. There was a big pot-bellied wood stove that heated the place, wooden floors, and most important for me at the time, shelves of candy. Old George seemed to relish having us come in, as he always grabbed a big bowl of candy, lowered it so that we could see, and after a minute, he would say "Take plenty."

This seemed too good to be true, so with big eyes and thoughts of the sweet stuff, I would reach for as many pieces as my little hand could grab. But then George would say, "Take one!" I was always surprised when he said that, and a little disappointed and humbled with my one piece of candy!

# EVENING GHOSTS

After the long daylight hours of June and July, it seemed like summer would never end, but now it was August and the days were growing shorter. The evening darkness was exciting and also a little scary, so I didn't like to be outdoors when it was dark.

One day, I stayed out a little later than usual but managed to get home before dark to find Mom busy hanging the last of her laundry outside.

It was a big affair when Mom did laundry, especially the sheets, and she had plenty of girls to help with the colored clothes. It took a lot of water that she heated up on the big cooking stove in the kitchen. She had a wringer washer and several galvanized washtubs for rinsing. Finally, she would take the clothes out to dry on the clothesline behind the house.

I went inside and sat on the bottom step of the staircase which seemed huge and for some reason always gave me trouble. It took me extra time to climb onto that big step and then continue up the regular steps. I noticed no one else was around and I got scared, so I climbed the stairs. The only light I could see came from downstairs so it was getting darker as I kept going up. When I reached the top step, I saw something white moving ever so slowly, and it kept moving. I panicked, stepped back, lost my footing, and down the stairs I tumbled!

Mom had come back into the house just in time to watch me tumbling down. I hit the last step, the big step, and I somehow managed to land sitting straight up. We were both surprised! I told her about the ghosts upstairs. The ghosts were actually the sheets she had hung to dry upstairs where the windows at both ends of the house were open to catch the evening breeze.

## MORE EVENING GHOSTS

It was another August evening and the darkness still gave me the creeps. Looking out at the brightly lit neighboring houses made the darkness seem even darker. I liked it when everyone was safely home. This particular night they were, and I was minding my own business when Bing called out to me to go check the front porch. I didn't think twice, I just headed outside through our inner door, past the entranceway with shelves for storage, boots and stuff.

The outside porch was well lit with a single light at the entrance. I stood there, looking up and down the road to see if there was anyone out there. No one was in sight, so I started back into the house and through the entrance way, when I noticed one of the water buckets was slowly moving along the floor! The bucket was between the inner door and me. At first, I froze, and then I started screaming. By that time, Bing and Birdie were laughing hard. Mom came and caught them scaring the daylights out of me.

## MRS. ANTHONY and the BEARS

During winter, Holy Cross Village seemed a lot quieter. The snow covered the gardens and the birch trees were bare. One Sunday, after a busy morning of Mass, breakfast, and then a more relaxed schedule, our neighbor, Mrs. Anthony, came running to our front door, very upset. She was talking so fast that Mom couldn't understand her. She was saying something about bears, and so Mom invited her in and followed her to our living room window where they could see the hill by the Mission.

Mrs. Anthony pointed toward two figures gliding down the hill and insisted they were bears. When Mom had a chance to take a good look, she started laughing. When she could stop, she told Mrs. Anthony that they were Sisters and they were skiing down the hill.

It must have been quite a sight, with tall and commanding Sister Mary Ida,* covered in black veils and a cloak that resembled fur. Keeping up with her was Sister Mary Jude, who was round and short. Mom reminded Mrs. Anthony, "It can't be bears, because they hibernate during the winter."

*The Sisters of Saint Ann commonly include "Mary" in the first part of their religious names. The formal written convention for these names is to indicate the word "Mary" with just an initial, example: "Sister Mary Ida," but in these stories the religious names have been spelled out to eliminate confusion.

## MOM and DAD'S ANNIVERSARY

One summer, Mom and Dad had a huge celebration in honor of their wedding anniversary. Word got out to everyone in the village, including the Sisters and the priests who liked Mom and Dad. Sister Mary Ida, who was the cook for the Mission, was asked to bake a cake large enough for everyone in the community to have a piece. Sister Mary Ida gathered eggs from anyone who could spare them. The cake had four layers, was beautifully frosted and had a candle on the top representing Mom and Dad. The cake was simply amazing and I remember how excited Mom and Dad were for the celebration.

There was enough food prepared to feed everyone. There was excitement in the air as people filed by our house for coffee or tea and cake. Afterwards, people made their way to the hall for music and dancing.

The community hall had been prepared for a dance and we had square dancing for the first part of the evening. All of the kids knew how to dance; we simply followed the person calling out commands like, "Honor your partner, honor your corner!" Bing tried his hand at shouting out commands, standing on a bench, and there were several men who took turns being the caller. Everything was going great, but when the boys and girls went different directions in the dance, I was making my way through the moves when suddenly Tootie appeared, going the wrong way. There was nothing to do but keep dancing, but I couldn't help but laugh. Bing was watching and laughing so hard; everyone was having such a great time and no one cared. Later in the evening, when the square dancing was over, it was time for the Sadish (Schottische), the two step, and the waltz.

The record player we were using was owned by one of the bachelors who was a nice enough fellow, but not popular with the ladies. When he had asked a number of girls to dance and was turned down every time, he'd had enough and went and shut off the electric power which came from the village powerhouse. Some people went to check on what had happened and learned of his problem. It was decided that the girls all had to accept his invitations. Problem solved, and the dance went on.

It was so much fun to be part of it all. We loved it that little kids were treated as though we were an important part of the community.

# PARTNERS

One summer it was decided that the people of the village would do the "Partners Tradition." It meant nothing to me when I was told that I had a partner. It started with a knock at the door and who should appear but Frankie Turner. He was a young man, older and taller than me, and he seemed to fill the doorway. I was immediately intimidated. He had curly hair and I didn't like that, so I shied away from him. He just smiled as Mom introduced him to me as my partner and told me that, as my partner, Frankie would soon accompany me to the community hall for a dinner and dancing.

The day of the dance came and Frankie walked me to the hall where, sure enough, other people were already gathered for the sharing of food and dancing. After the meal, I escaped Frankie and joined my friends for the square dancing. The evening was fun and when it ended, Frankie made sure I was safely home. Days later, Frankie again knocked on the door to see me and this time he had a box of candy. Again, I grew shy in front of him, but Mom scolded me and told me to take the box and thank him. I grabbed the box and ran upstairs.

I think the Partners Tradition was meant as a way to teach older kids and younger kids to respect and look out for each other.

# LIFE ON THE RIVER

The St. Francis *and the* St. Joseph *on the Tanana River, circa 1942. Nick and his father Ephrem built the* St. Francis. *Back L-R Nick, Nellie and Manny; front L-R Joanne, Lolly, Bing, Sam and Eva. These were the first generation of boats used by Nick and Nellie's new business, Demientieff Navigation Company.*

## *OUR BOATS*
*by Samuel S. Demientieff*

*Dad became a river freighter after he'd been working for the miners in Flat in the 1930s. The story I heard him tell was that as he worked, he figured out how much he was making and could estimate how much income his season would bring.*

*During this time, he and mom got married and both of them were working for the miners. In his off hours, Dad also sold meat* the miners needed for their crews, so he figured out a plan to go to as many miners as possible and contract with them to sell them meat, fish or whatever he could bring in. Talking with miners about this, he learned he could make more money being a hunter selling meat than his regular job was bringing in, so he set up the food contracts he needed and quit his job. His boss was disappointed because Dad was a good worker, but he understood what Dad was doing.

Then Dad needed to have a good boat and barge, and I believe his dad, Ephrem, helped him build the first outfit.

There was a larger barge service operating, called Day Navigation Company. The owner, Clyde Day, had three shallow draft boats and barges, but the Iditarod area was depleted and the mining work came from Flat, a town eight miles into the hills, where Dad was setting up his contracts. Day could see his operation slowly shutting down and he began selling out. That is when Dad as a new operator began hauling what was required for the new, smaller mining operations.

The boats used during this time were primarily the Beaver and the Sea Wolf. The barges we used with these boats had differing load capacities, but were all deck barges, which means all freight was hauled on top of their flat decks.

I was a young kid during the Second World War, when my dad saw the opportunity to carry construction materials and military cargo for the new airfields along the Yukon. Our 90-ton barge, the St. Francis, was built on the banks of the Chena in the Fairbanks town area. A photo of this boat says it was purchased for $1000. We have a picture of the St. Francis, just after it was launched, and I remember I had to jump onto the deck after the launch to tie it up. On the trip up the Yukon to Rampart, we were on the St. Francis.

Dad rented a place in Fairbanks and we spent a winter there early in the 1940s. I remember seeing Life magazines with war pictures, so maybe it was around 1944 or 45. The St. Francis and St. Joseph were used in the new business known as Demientieff Navigation Company. We have pictures of the two boats bringing *a government house down the Yukon in 1943. There were probably small kicker type boats, too, but those were just used for travel and personal transportation.*

The Beaver *pushing two barges, tied up to take on water on the Tanana River below Manley Hot Springs.*

*Tiny's river memories start with the* Beaver *and the* Sea Wolf. *My parents bought the* Sea Wolf *in 1948. A sternwheeler database for Alaska says it was built in Holikachuk in 1939. The* Sea Wolf *was a gasoline-powered sternwheeler, made for running the Innoko and Iditarod rivers, so it was narrow and long: 54 feet long. The Iditarod boats were specially constructed for the river bends that twisted back and forth, coming back so close that in two places the river ran into itself and created a short cut, called a "cut off." The old goldrush town of Iditarod is located on a cut off, making the town isolated from the running river. Anyway, one can see from the map how close the Iditarod River comes back in the direction of Holy Cross.*

*I can't remember the summer we bought the* Beaver, *our smaller boat, but we had it before we bought the* Sea Wolf. *It had been a US government boat, made for use by the US Fish and Wildlife Service. We bought it in Rampart, on the Yukon. The* Beaver *had a big diesel with a large propeller located in a tunnel that Dad designed to increase horsepower and allow the boat to operate in shallow water.*

On the Sea Wolf, *the gas motor was located in the front part of the boat, connected to the chain drives in the rear. The stern wheel at the back of the boat was chain driven. With the motor in front and the chain drives in the rear, a long shaft was required. It was held in place with self-aligning bearings all the way to the back.*

*On our journeys up to Iditarod, we stopped many times at Holikachuk, picking up stuff for the long trip from Old Man Walker's store. We were able to see some old riverboats parked in a slough. I think one was called the* Anna Belle *or* Clara Belle.

*On occasions, a chain would break on the* Sea Wolf, *so we would have to stop and dig out the long chain, repair it and reassemble it. I remember after we had owned and operated the* Sea Wolf *for some years, on one trip down the Tanana River we had three barges, fully loaded. The* Beaver *was attached to the side of the* Sea Wolf. *With all that extra load, the sternwheel sheared all of its spokes! So, it was broken down. Dad, I think, knew that we would have to be changing the spokes, but didn't expect the break down. In our family stories about that trip we named an island "Fourth of July Island" because the spokes sheared there on that day.*

*Around 1950, we built sponsons—additions to the hull of the* Sea Wolf—*to make it about five feet total wider. That improved the look of the* Sea Wolf *and made it much more stable. We later purchased a narrow shallow draft barge that was made to work on the Innoko and Iditarod rivers.*

*Many times, some of us kids were off the boats because of some accident or something else, like the start of school, or not being able to get back up river before the river froze over. We were always early to check out of school in the spring because my folks wanted to make as many trips as possible, and then we were usually the last outfit off of the river in the fall, too, so us kids were late to school. Our life on the river was always an adventure. We saw many animals: birds, bears, moose. We saw forest fires, and the last of the big steamboats. It was just an amazing life. I was the last boy in our family of ten children and there were five girls after me, so there were stories and experiences the younger ones did not have. As the older ones left, the younger ones had their experiences. This is where Tiny begins her river stories.*

Sea Wolf *hooked up to 90 ton deck barge built by Nick Demientieff.*

*On one trip, Manny saved a young moose calf from drowning, pulling it into the kicker boat. The cow moose was very unhappy. There was time for one photo before Manny shoved the calf out on a sandbar so the mother moose would not charge them (Sam Demientieff story).*

# MAPS

## YUKON MOUTH to GALENA

*Nick and Nellie Demientieff and family—Demientieff Navigation—1930s–1960s*

# LIFE ON THE RIVER

## RUBY to FAIRBANKS

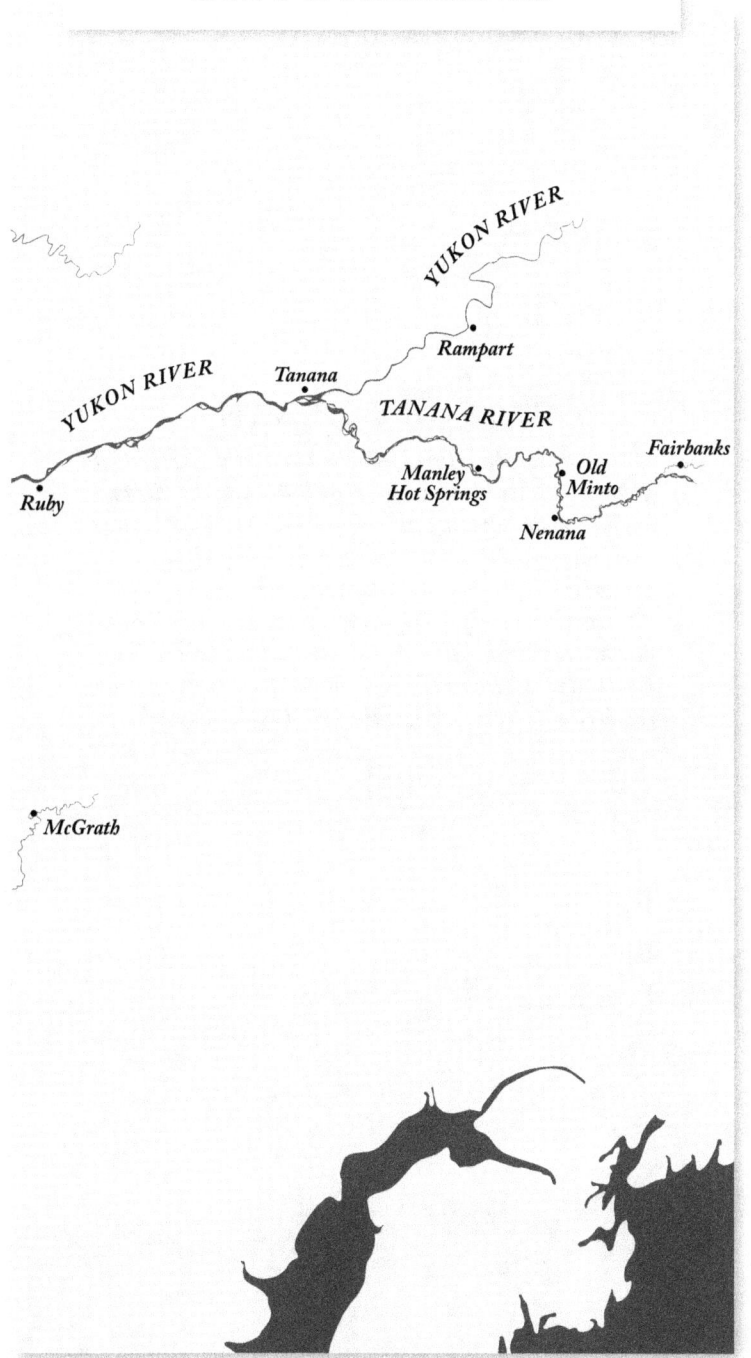

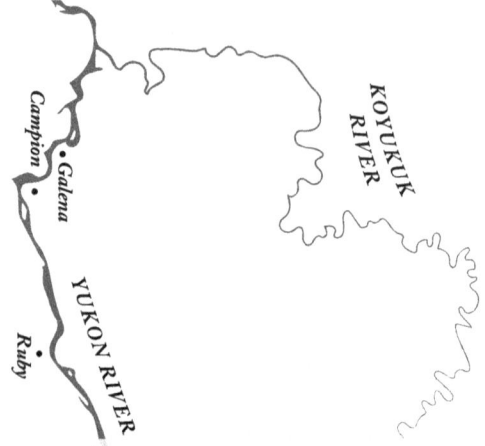

## GALENA to NENANA

*During World War II and following years, the Demientieff family's boats and barges were busy delivering supplies and building materials along the Yukon River. Much of the cargo was military-related. The Demientieff's main freighting run was to load at Nenana and unload at Galena, where a 1941–42 airfield was built as a refueling stop for lend-lease aircraft destined for Siberia. After the war and into the 1950s, the air force bases at Galena and Campion continued to expand and employ the river freighters for the delivery of heavy goods.*

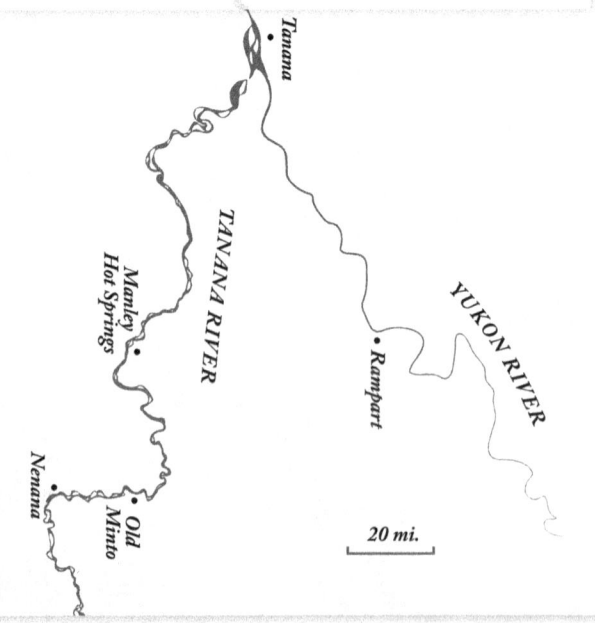

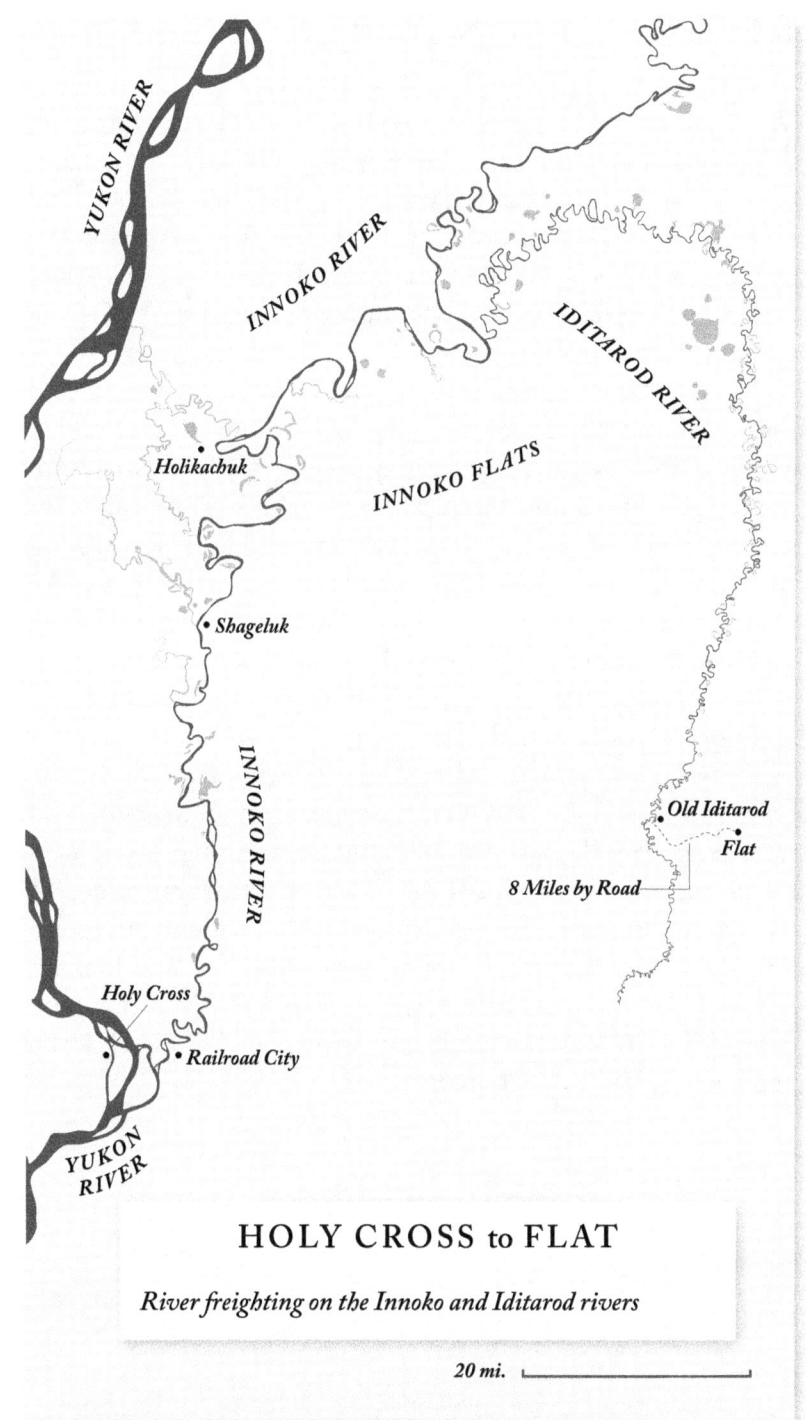

**HOLY CROSS to FLAT**

*River freighting on the Innoko and Iditarod rivers*

20 mi.

# RIVER ADVENTURES

Mom and Dad had started their own river freighting business in the early 1930s, which was a rather unusual occupation in those early days for Alaska Natives, but Dad was a determined man. He had his hands full overseeing the operations of his outfit and his crew while they did the loading and unloading of freight, the sounding of the river depths, the tying up at village docks.

I think Mom had the tougher job, however, as she cooked meals for our family of ten and Dad's crew. This entailed cooking from scratch every day, every meal, always with homemade bread and biscuits. She was also responsible for keeping track of us, and since we were all like Dad—strong spirited—it added to Mom's challenges in raising us. We younger kids were to "stay clear of operations, help Mom, and watch your step!" It amazed me, as I'm sure it did most of the people in the villages, that we all grew up to adulthood and none of us drowned.

Between visits to the villages and towns, our life on the river was mostly quiet. Once we shoved off from shore and were underway, there was time to mull over thoughts and new memories. It wasn't so quiet for Mom, who always seemed to have something she had to do, but remained patient, quiet, and kind. Dad was usually in the pilothouse of the *Sea Wolf*, looking out over the boats, the barges, the river, and the ever-changing countryside. It was his life, being with his wife, his children and friends. It was his domain.

# The PILOTHOUSE of the *SEA WOLF*

When I was on the *Sea Wolf*, I would climb up to my bunk, which was huge. I'd find a comic book, take a nap and settle back into the rhythm of the river. Naturally after a nap I was full of energy and things to do. Sometimes I ventured out on my own to explore the barge, check out the paddlewheel, or spend time in the pilothouse.

*Nellie, Nick, and Tiny in doorway of the* **Sea Wolf**, *at Nenana dock.*

One day I decided to climb up on top of the pilothouse. I climbed the ladder to the second level, walked past Mom and Dad's cabin and Lolly's cabin, then up the next ladder to the third level. It had never crossed my mind before how high up that was. I had just wanted to see what it was like. I carefully crawled along until I reached the front of the pilothouse roof. The view was amazing. I could see far in front of the barge, the flag waving, the river current and the eddies swirling about. Waves were created in the wake of our boat as we slowly but steadily moved along.

It was strangely quiet up there on the roof. Now and then an echo rolled across the river and seemed to bounce back. The return sound was more faint, still the same sound but dissolving and fading away. After a while, I inched forward on my belly and hung my head over to look at Dad. It didn't take long for him to notice me. He rang the bell for Mom and I knew what that meant. My poor Mom. It seemed that even with all she had to do, she could still now and then get scolded on my behalf! All she would tell me, not hollering or yelling, but in a firm voice, was, "You mustn't do that!" I couldn't help but notice that she said "mustn't,"—must not—okay, I must not do that. I agree, I mustn't do that. I won't do it anymore. She got her point across.

When we traveled downriver, there was excitement in the air. We moved faster going with the current rather than against it, and likely we went faster when we were going on a new job. Each trip was different; each time I noticed things that I hadn't noticed before, or perhaps it was because I was growing older and becoming more aware of things.

## The PADDLEWHEEL

After a busy visit to one of the villages, I liked to stand in front of the pilothouse and watch as we pulled away. Dad would call out directions to the crew like "Pull the plank, untie the ropes…" and then we'd shove off to the next village.

Usually, friends or relatives would be standing on the riverbank, seeing us off. We would wave until we could no longer see each other. Sometimes I was glad, thinking about the next village and the people; sometimes I was sad to leave the one we were in.

From time to time on a sunny day, I would take my pillow, climb the ladder and head for the back deck of the *Sea Wolf* to lie in the sun. This was my getaway. I'd lay in the sunshine, gaze at the blue skies and the beautiful clouds. I would think about how fortunate I was to have Mom and Dad, all my brothers and sisters, so many friends and relatives, and traveling on the river. I felt safe, happy and loved.

**Beaver** *and* **Sea Wolf** *preparing to haul barge loads of equipment from Nenana to Galena on the Yukon.*

I would roll over onto my stomach, rest my chin on my hands, and watch the paddlewheel steadily turning and the water churning, as droplets of water splashed all around. My eyes followed the motion down to the river where the churned-up water folded into a huge wave, creating a ripple on each side of the big paddlewheel. The ripples fanned out and drifted off; the big rolling waves gave way to smaller waves and went out of sight. I loved to watch the same thing over and over until I was relaxed and peaceful. It was as if the river, with the paddlewheel turning and churning, took my worries and mixed them all up, and then they slowly faded away.

**Beaver** *and kicker boat pulled up alongside the* **Sea Wolf,** *visible just behind.*

## The *BEAVER*

Once in a while we just used the *Beaver* and docked the *Sea Wolf*. The *Beaver* was the smaller but more powerful of the two boats and we used it to go up the smaller rivers. I liked the *Beaver* because it was not as high and tall as the *Sea Wolf*, so we were closer to the river water.

The inside layout of the *Beaver* was different than the *Sea Wolf*. There was the engine area, then further back on the left side was the galley and a makeshift living and eating area. The table, when it wasn't in use, could be folded up onto the wall and secured with a latch. On each side of the boat there were two door-like openings with sliding doors. In the middle was a long bench. The small kitchen area had a wood stove, shelving and storage. Behind and next to the stove was a doorway to the bathroom. On the opposite side was the bunkroom. Unlike the huge built-in bunks of the *Sea Wolf*, the beds were canvas cots, suspended by large chains that hung from the ceiling.

I loved the sliding doors to the outside, especially the one by the kitchen. It was open most of the time so there was always fresh air and the river water was so close at hand. When Mom needed water to wash the dishes or do some cleaning, she simply scooped some water from the river and put the dishpan on the stove.

One day, I decided to fetch some water using Mom's dishpan. I got it down and walked over to the open door and leaned out. I noticed how different it was when leaning out; the wind was strong and the water was moving by very fast. I took the pan and lowered it into the river, trying to fill it with water. It didn't take very long before it was too heavy and I couldn't lift it back out. In fact, it could have pulled me overboard, so I had to let it go. I will never forget the moment of letting it go. I imagined it sinking down into the depths, never to return.

## The BEAR on the *BEAVER*

One summer day as we were returning upriver, we took time to dock and get a good night's sleep. Dad and Mom slept in their cabin, Lolly in hers, us kids in our bunks on the *Sea Wolf*. Bing, Birdie, and the crew were sleeping on the other boat, the *Beaver*.

It was early the next morning when I heard an urgent whisper, Lolly calling, "Dad." It was quiet and then she called again, "Dad!" and once again, her voice a little louder, "Dad!" Finally, he woke up and answered her, "What is it?"

She said, "There's a bear on the *Beaver*!"

There was a huge bear walking along the narrow catwalk

that ran from the front of the boat to the back of the boat. It was inching along, holding on to brace itself.

Dad told Lolly to try to wake up the boys who were in the cabin, located on the second floor of the *Beaver* and not too far away.

**Beaver** *pushing a barge on the Yukon. Manny is on the right in the kicker boat.*

Then Dad told Lolly to go ahead and shoot it. Lolly had her own gun and was a sharp shooter. She did shoot, only the bear managed to get back to the bow of the boat. When the second shot rang out, down went the bear with most of its body hanging over the river. That was a problem. By then Dad had his pants on and was trying to get over to the *Beaver*, which meant that he had to climb down the ladder, cross over to the barge and onto the bow of the *Beaver*.

And then the bear, with a simple kick of its leg, slipped into the river.

# BIRDIE'S a BOY

Mom took particular pride in her children and she enjoyed watching how people liked to see our family when we visited in villages. Birdie was just a little boy then, a skinny kid with long, thick, curly hair. He could be shy when fussing older women paid too much attention to him, and he'd want to disappear behind Mom.

*Sam, holding guitar, with brothers and friends in days on the river Sam says were surely "even better than Huck Finn."*

One spring, when we tied up for a visit at a village, one of the women came down to the boat to visit and she had a present for Birdie. Mom called out to Birdie and he shyly came forward. The woman proudly presented him with a little brown cardboard box. As the woman watched, Mom helped Birdie open it. It was a beautiful little tea set, which surprised Mom and made Birdie burst out in tears. The woman thought Birdie was a little girl with his long curly hair. Dad was beside himself and instructed Mom to get his hair cut: "Birdie's a boy!"

# IRENE the BAKER

Irene was two years older than me and very serious. I don't remember her ever getting into mischief. On the boats, traveling between villages, she would try her hand at baking. Her cakes and lemon meringue pies were simply wonderful. She used Sugar, Tootie and me as guinea pigs, the first ones to try out her new recipes.

One day, Irene got busy measuring, mixing and pouring the batter into the waiting floured cake pans and into the oven. She was always hoping that the non-stop vibrations of the engines would not ruin her delectable creations. She worked hard frosting the cake and it was beautiful. I remember waiting for the slice of delight, only when I took the first bite and started to chew, there was something wrong. I didn't know what, but was not interested in finding out. I spit out the cake and tried to rid myself of that awful experience. Irene stood in horror, not sure what to think. I asked her what kind of cake was that? "It's coffee cake," she said. Later, we learned her mistake was using coffee grounds, instead of a cup of coffee.

# The STOLEN BIRTHDAY

Traveling on the boat during the summer months must have been hectic for Mom, as she was cooking and baking not only for her family but also for Dad's crew, keeping an eye on us kids and the usual tasks of family life.

Out of our family of ten kids, six birthdays rolled around during the summer months with Sugar's the first, on the nineteenth of June.

Mom made a big deal out of birthdays. When she baked a cake she mixed in little things like a dime, a penny, or a little plastic ring, each wrapped in wax paper and put into the batter.

They were like finding little fortune cookies in the cake. The dime meant you would grow up to be rich, the penny meant you would be poor, and the ring meant marriage. Then she decorated the cake with candy sprinkles and candles. She made sure we each had a couple of presents and when the candles were lit, we'd sing the birthday song.

*Some Demientieff kids and friends on board a Yukon River barge.*

One June, I think I was about six or seven years old, I remember thinking about the fact that my younger sister Sugar's birthday was on a similar number than mine but in a different month. Mine was on the eighteenth of August and Sugar's was the nineteenth of June—coming right up. As Mom busied herself with the cake and wrapping the gifts, I decided to claim June nineteenth as my birthday. Mom was so busy she didn't notice. For me the day was great! The cake, little fortune cookies, the presents, and the happy tune of the old birthday song were so exciting. I beamed and enjoyed every moment. I pulled it off; I don't know what possessed me, just childhood mischief.

No one noticed, then as July faded away and August approached, Mom started off with Tootie's birthday, then as each special day clicked by, the other August birthday was finally coming up. Mom knew it was coming, but there were so many birthdays to keep track of!

I remember that when Mom asked whose birthday it was, I quickly announced that it was mine, which was true this time, and the celebration began. I basked in another birthday! Sugar, in frustration, asked when was it going to be her day. I do remember a feeling of guilt, but I don't remember what happened.

That memory bothered me off and on, so many years later, during a work trip to Fairbanks one June, I made a quick trip to a bakery, selected a beautiful cake and brought it to Sugar. When I brought out the cake and sang a quick version of Happy Birthday to her, she was so surprised and puzzled. I told her it was a long story, but that I had stolen her birthday once when we were kids. She didn't recall it, but was happy for the cake.

# PLAY TIME

We stopped at a lot of villages along the Yukon, including Tanana, Ruby, Galena, Nulato, Kaltag, Shageluk, Anvik, Holy Cross, and St. Mary's. While traveling on the river between villages, we kids spent a lot of time with each other. Sometimes Birdie would tell us stories or we would play games, do simple things together.

Thinking back to all the time we kids spent with each other, I believe that it provided time for us to grow closer. In the isolation of living on the boat, doing things together afforded us private family time. I know that I felt safe and lucky to have so many brothers and sisters. Sometimes in the villages we were challenged by a few village kids who wanted to taunt or pick on us, but our older brothers and sisters always looked out for us younger ones. I knew I could rely on them—I still do.

# TIME OFF

One time, we had just delivered a load after a long trip. The work was done and Dad released the crew. He didn't allow drinking on board and it just happened to be a nice hot day. Most of the crew disappeared into the village except this one guy who was a little older than the others and a friendly guy. He noticed Birdie, Sugar, Tootie and me sitting on the deck of the *Sea Wolf* and told us that he was going to celebrate with this one can of beer he'd saved for himself.

While this guy was gone to get his beer, Birdie instructed us, "If he asks you to get a can opener, say, 'No.' Tell him to get it himself."

The guy returned with his precious can and was savoring just the idea of the taste. Sure enough, he asked one of us to get the opener from the kitchen and we each refused.

He went into the boat and while he was gone, Birdie grabbed the can and started to shake it, then we all took a turn. In a minute or two the fellow was back and we were all sitting there looking innocent. When he drove the opener into the can it was almost as if the thing had exploded. Foamy beer shot up and sprayed everywhere. The poor guy was so stunned, and we took off running in all directions. He chased after us but we knew the boat and barge too well to be found.

*View of a bend in Iditarod River, with the gold rush town of Iditarod in distance. Many of Iditarod's commercial and residential buildings had been moved to the nearby town of Flat by the 1930s. Lomen Brothers Photograph Collection, 1903–1930, at the Alaska State Library.*

# TRAVELING the INNOKO RIVER to FLAT

Now and then Dad had to make a run to the town of Flat. Back in the day, Flat was a thriving mining town that looked very much like the set of an old cowboy Western movie.

In order to get to Flat, Dad took the boats up the Innoko River, which had clear water instead of silt, and was not as wide as either the Tanana or Yukon rivers. The landscape was different, too. Rather than rolling hills covered in the green leaves of the white birch trees, there were cottonwood trees and the Iditarod Flats. As we moved along the river, I could see the shoreline. It was quite a ways off but clearly visible. Sometimes it was necessary to travel closer to the deeper side of the river and then I could clearly see rose bushes, highbush cranberry bushes, goose grass and other plants.

I remember that I was in the boat, perhaps having lunch, when the bell rang. This was a signal to come out of the boat. So, we all made our way out, either to the barge or up the ladder and out on the deck. I climbed the ladder along with Irene, Sugar and Tootie. Everyone was quiet, uncertain why Dad had rung the bell.

I looked up to see Dad watching out over the river and maneuvering the wooden sternwheel that drove the boat—slowly, quietly and skillfully. We were entering the Innoko Flats. The Innoko widened and there was tall grass growing out of the shallow waters that seemed to go on forever. In this clearing, the sky seemed so much bigger.

Mom was just as curious as the rest of us. Dad spoke softly to her and then reached up over his head to sound the horn. Mounted on top of the pilothouse, the horn was quite loud, and when the sound of the horn trumpeted, there was an echo that seemed to roll on over and over. As suddenly as the sound broke the silence, a huge flock of geese rose from the tall grass. There were so many that they darkened the sky. Some flew off to the right, others to the left, and it was impossible to count them. It was a sight to behold! I believe Dad was the most excited one of us, to be able to quietly enter the Flats and then share the wildlife in all its glory with us.

From the Innoko Flats we turned up the twisty Iditarod River. Finally, we reached our destination, the Iditarod Landing, with Flat a few miles away by road. Once the boats were secured, Dad walked down the gangplank with us younger girls running along by his side, trying to keep up with his swift, long strides. He was headed to a lone building nearby. No one was around when we got there but there was a phone mounted on the outside of the building. It was one of those old phones with a mouthpiece sticking out, two little bells above the mouthpiece, and a handle that Dad had to crank to get the phone working. It was the system that was set up to notify someone back in the town of Flat that a boat had landed.

While we waited for a ride to come for us from Flat, there was time enough to return to the boat and prepare to go into town. Mom got herself ready and us kids did the same. It wasn't as exciting as arriving at a village where kids and dogs were waiting and the people were all waving. This landing was quiet, so the excitement was in getting ready for the town visit.

After a short while, a car arrived for us. It was a jalopy, looking very much like one in the comics. It even had an open rumble seat with just enough room for Sugar, Tootie and me. Mom and Dad sat with the driver and we drove off to town.

Sea Wolf *pushing a barge up the twisting Iditarod River, kids in foreground.*

# TOOTSIE CROSBIE

In Flat, Mom wanted to visit her friend Tootsie Crosbie. The trips to Flat were not as frequent as those along the Tanana or Yukon, so I didn't recall who this Tootsie was, but she had a nice house. The front door opened and there stood a woman who smiled and welcomed Mom and Dad. It was the first time I'd seen a colored person and it was shocking. She was friendly and happy to see us, and Mom and Dad were happy to see her. Sugar, Tootie and I stuck close to Mom.

We made our way into her home and it was beautiful. There was a warm, inviting kitchen where she put a pot of water on for tea, then took us on a tour—the kitchen, the bathroom and a sitting room. I was amazed at all of the finery: doilies on the furniture, on the tables and everywhere. Lastly, she opened a door to her bedroom and we were all able to enter at once. There was a huge bed covered with a fine quilt, and on top of each of the four wooden bedposts there were wigs of hair! They were all different colors, which certainly caught my attention, and from that moment, I was on guard.

When Tootsie finished chatting with Mom and Dad, she came over to us kids. We were standing very close to each other and I remember feeling confused. The closer she came, the more we took steps back, back, until we hit the wall. Trapped, I just stood there not sure what was going to happen. Smiling, she just leaned over and touched my cheek, still talking to Mom and Dad, and then she returned to their visit.

Later on, I recalled that first time meeting with Tootsie and I asked Mom about her. Mom said she was a friend that had come to Alaska when the miners did.

After we moved to Fairbanks and years later when I was doing research for Black History Month, I came upon Tootsie's real name and a short history about her. I also learned that she was living in Fairbanks at a nursing home. I was living in Anchorage at the time, but when I was in Fairbanks, I would visit Tootsie. After all the years, and in her old age, she still remembered me, Mom, Dad and our visit.

## The FLAT SALOON

After the visit with Tootsie, we walked to the saloon, which reminded me of ones I had seen in Western movies. The wooden floor had an open area, maybe for dancing, and a huge wooden bar with high stools. The men sitting around the bar greeted Mom and Dad. I climbed up onto a high stool and leaned on the smooth wooden bar.

There was a long painting of a woman in a red dress with long black hair, bright red lips and a smile, laying on her side holding a cigarette in a long holder. The bartender came over to Mom and Dad and shook their hands, happily chatting. I was too taken up with everything from the brass fixtures, the glasses, and the huge selection of candy beneath the painting of the lady.

After chatting with Mom and Dad, the bartender came over to us kids. He was a friendly sort of fellow, and I think these people didn't have kids coming into the bar that often. I'm not sure what got my sister Tootie started, but she started to sing. I was surprised that she could actually sing! She belted out that old song, "Kookaburra." There she was with her blond hair in braids and her blue eyes, singing like she owned the place. Once she finished, the men hooted and hollered, clapping for her, asking for her to sing it again. This time, someone perched her up on the bar with her little legs dangling over the edge. She was a hit.

Then the bartender came back over to us kids and told us that maybe it was time for us to go back to the boats so Dad and Mom could stay to visit with their friends. I remember saying, "No, we aren't going without them." So, he said, "What would it take to change your minds?"

Looking at all that candy and the cans of shoestring potatoes, I motioned to the candy. He caught on quick and picked out some candy bars for each of us and brought them over, thinking that was it. But we kept on pointing to other bars of candy and ended up with a big bag of candy. Then we rode along the dirt road back to the boats. Sitting in that rumble seat, I looked up at the dark sky sprinkled with stars, breathed in fresh evening air, and life was good!

# LIFE IN FAIRBANKS

*Joanne, Irene, Sugar, Tiny and Tootie at the Chena River cabin near Fairbanks.*

# FAIRBANKS and CHANGE

As the lazy days of summer slipped away, our long hours of daylight shortened and the darkness of night came earlier. The warm sunshine began to cool and the winds grew stronger. It was subtle, but as the days of August clicked by, the leaves would turn from lush green to bright yellow, orange and rust.

I could feel the change and it was exciting. The wild wind would whip around quickly, change direction and make the leaves dance and the trees sway. Our river days were numbered for the fall season, and preparations for the coming winter were already on Dad's mind.

Dad and Mom had been doing the river freighting operation for a few years. They had decided to move the operation and our family to Fairbanks, where we kids could go to the public school during the winter months. Our new home was outside Fairbanks, on the banks of the Chena River. Dad and Mom bought land and built a large log cabin. Manny cleared a place where the boats could be pulled out of the river for the winter, away from the freezing river ice and the spring breakup.

The cabin was cozy with Mom's cooking stove and a wood stove fashioned from an oil drum to provide heating for the house. Dad and the boys dug deep into the ground and tapped into well water. He put a hand pump next to a window in the kitchen. It took a while to prime it, but when the water started to flow it was cold, clean, sparkling and clear. There were partitions to separate the living room and kitchen from the sleeping areas. I say sleeping areas because we didn't have bedrooms with walls; we had curtains for privacy. Mom and Dad had their area, and next were the bunk beds for Tootie and me and all the girls. There was a wall to separate the girls' room from the boys' room.

Out behind the cabin, Mom had a network of clotheslines strung about between the trees in the back yard. Dad built a sandbox for us younger ones, and of course there was the outhouse.

**Sea Wolf** and Beaver *at the Demientieff's Chena River landing at Fairbanks, near the family house. Encouraged by our father, Nick, young Manny did the land-clearing for boat landing and road with a D-8 cat (Sam Demientieff).*

Life here felt very different from our Holy Cross home, where the houses were fairly close and everyone knew everyone. There, the kids walked to school together, the teachers were Sisters, and we all prayed and studied together. There was a sense of community there, a place where we all belonged and were friends. In Fairbanks, our house had no one living close by; we were away from the city, connected by roads. We didn't have a phone, but we had a television.

In Holy Cross, people walked everywhere and it wasn't necessary to have a car, just a truck to do the hauling. In Fairbanks, we needed a car to drive to town, check the mail, shop, and for just getting around.

# SCHOOL

Every school day we walked up our dirt road to the main road and waited for the big yellow school bus. One day while we waited, Irene checked with Sugar and me to see if we knew who we were. She asked me my name and I answered "Tiny" and she said "No, it's Nellie Demientieff." All this time, I thought Tiny was my real name!

Then she turned to Sugar and asked her name. Sugar responded, "Nick E. Demientieff!" Irene and I both burst out laughing, informing her that it was Dad's name, that *she* was Shirley Frances Demientieff.

We rode the bus to school together, but once there, I was singled out and informed that I was going to be transferred to a brand-new school in south Fairbanks, Hunter Elementary School. This time I was going on by myself. By this time, I was getting used to changes and learning to go along without too much fuss.

My school in Fairbanks was a public school with both men and women as teachers and no religious instruction. There were no Native kids in my class, so I felt alone. At first, we were all strangers, but as the school year went by, I made two friends. I never met the parents of my new schoolmates, though. In Holy Cross we had known all the kids and their parents.

# The CITY

In Fairbanks, there were stores spread across the town. There was a bakery, the Northern Commercial Company store, cafés and restaurants, the little church across the bridge, St. Joseph's Hospital, bars, and two movie theaters. In Holy Cross, we'd had only one store, owned by George Turner. It had everything people needed, from nails to candy. It was a new way of life for us in Fairbanks, where the people were mainly white.

There were many firsts that year. It would be my first time going to a bakery. Birdie was old enough to drive, and he asked me if I wanted to go along with him to the bakery. I wasn't quite sure what that was, but once there, I couldn't believe my eyes. There in the showcase were cookies and things I never saw before. He asked me if I'd ever had a crème puff before. I said no, and he bought each of us one. So, we each had a big puffy thing filled with cream. It was so good.

The Empress Theatre had a promotion called "Space Cadets" to get customers, especially kids, into the shows on Saturdays. All we needed to get into the movies was a bread bag from the Sunshine Bakery. We worked poor Mom over to get enough bags for us.

Finally, Saturday arrived and off to the theater we went. Once inside, we found our seats. In the village, we sat on long wooden benches, but here in the city we each had our own seat and it was very comfortable. The movie hall in Holy Cross was an old Quonset hut, set on a concrete foundation. Here, the walls were painted with beautiful artwork, the ceiling had a few twinkling lights, and there was a huge curtain hiding the movie screen. Once the music started, the curtains opened magically and the screen lit up.

First there were ads, short little things. I clearly remember the one where a matador appeared with a smiling bull. The jingle was, "Candy, I like candy! It comes in handy when I fight de bull!" Of course, I wanted candy!

*The Empress Theatre in Fairbanks, 1952. Built in 1927, the theater had just been re-modeled in the early 1950s with this large neon-lit marquee. It closed in 1953. Photo from cinematreasures.org.*

I remember the movie being scary. I wasn't expecting that, and when a monster appeared I crawled beneath my seat. I don't remember how long I had been under there until Irene missed me and called out my name. She scolded me to get up into my seat and stay there. So, I leaned up against the back of my seat and kept my eyes closed during most of the show. We were now officially Space Cadets!

## OUR NEIGHBORHOOD GROCERY STORE

One evening, Sugar, Tootie, and I walked to the APG to buy some candy. APG was the Airport Grocery Store—we had shortened its name. When our shopping was done, we were walking and talking, taking our dear old time going home. Then we heard the sounds of a small airplane drawing closer and closer. Suddenly we saw the plane, flying close to the tree tops. We had never seen that before and my imagination went wild, thinking it might be the Japanese! In the early 1950s, the Second World War was still close in our minds.

We ran, hiding among the trees and making our way home while the plane kept flying back and forth. We finally made it home and ran to Mom, all talking at once, pointing and gesturing, "Mom it's the Japanese!" She stood there trying to make sense of what we were saying and then turned on the radio to see if there was news. Later on, we learned that a crop duster was flying in the area spraying mosquitoes.

One day when Irene was not feeling well, Mom brought her to the doctor only to learn that she had hepatitis. It was going to be a very long recovery and she was confined to her bed. That must have been very difficult for her; I know it would have been for me.

When we were home by ourselves one afternoon, she asked me to walk to the APG. She gave me money and instructed me to get her some 7Up. I took the money and went to the store, over a mile away, which took some time. When I got to the store there were all kinds of pop: Orange Crush, Bubble Up, 7Up—but it was Sparkling Water that I noticed. So instead of the 7Up, I bought the Sparkling Water, something new and wonderful. When I gave the bottle to her, she glanced at it and tried it. Something was wrong. Her face grimaced and she looked at the bottle. What's this? I took a taste and she was right, it was terrible, especially after anticipating the sweet, savory, bubbly 7Up.

A few days went by and once again Irene and I were alone. This time she wanted milk. Now what could go wrong with choosing milk? She gave me the money and instructions. I walked again to the APG, looked over the selection and noticed buttermilk. Wow, that sounded great! I bought a carton, trying to imagine what this buttermilk was going to taste like. I proudly gave it to Irene and again she tasted it and again her face immediately changed. She spit it out! She looked at the carton and read "Buttermilk." That was the end of my shopping for her.

# BEING SICK

I had a hard time my first year in the public school. I caught every communicable disease that found its way among the kids. It seemed like just as soon as I recovered from one sickness, I would fall victim to another. It was like clockwork. I'd have to report to the school nurse, who in turn would bring me home in a taxi, carry me into the house and lay me down on Mom's big black steamer trunk. The nurse would give Mom instructions on what to feed me, and so forth.

The first year in Fairbanks, I missed so much school that I had to start over in the same grade.

One time when I was sick and laid up in bed, Dad came to see me. I didn't quite know what to do. He took off his hat, held it in his hands and came quietly over to me like I was something important, like some kind of princess.

I was scared, and he asked, "Are you going to live?" I was so surprised—I had to think about that. After a short period of silence, I responded in a weakened voice, "I think so." And I did. How endearing!

# WINTER FUN

Winter in the Interior was very long, dark and cold. Since we were away from the city lights out at the cabin, the night skies were still beautiful, with twinkling stars, northern lights and a bright moon. Sometimes the moonlight was so bright it left shadows on the snow that twinkled as well. The winter months seemed longer than the short months of summer.

Dad built an ice-skating rink on the river. After dinner we would often put on our skates and spend the evening playing Crack the Whip, racing, and having fun.

One winter, Mom and Dad were all excited about an upcoming event. It was the first satellite in space!

Dad told us kids, as we headed out to ice skate, that when he hollered, we should lie down on the ice and look up at the sky where we would be able to see the Sputnik satellite. Sure enough, moving slowly across the dark skies and among the stars traveled the first satellite.

Our eldest brother, Manny, seemed to fit right into Fairbanks. He was a handsome young man. He knew how to sing and play guitar and he was a happy, friendly guy. Manny's friends liked to come to our house and make music together. It was fun. Birdie and Bing also made friends quite easily and brought them home to hang around the house as well.

Manny had a team of dogs that he trained and worked. He fussed over the dogs, cooking for them and taking them out to run and race. His hard work paid off when he won several dog races and skijoring (skiing while pulled by a dog) competitions. He also won the hearts of several of the ladies!

*Manny with dog team, our mother Nellie at his left. In that year, he ran his team in the Junior division of the North American Dog Mushing Championships, during the Fairbanks Winter Carnival.*

When Sugar, Tootie and I got a little older, we would help Manny out with cooking the dog food. He would start out with water, oats, chunks of dry fish and other stuff. He kept the fire going as the dog stew cooked. When the aroma of the dry fish was just too tempting, I recall the three of us younger ones being drawn to the "dog pot" and fishing out pieces of the hot savory stuff. Irene caught us snacking, and put an end to that.

*Tiny and her dog Corky were the winners of a one-dog race at the Birch Hill track near Fairbanks.*

# INDOOR FUN

Irene kept an eye on Sugar, Tootie and me. Maybe it was out of boredom that she started making plans for us. We had a green chalkboard hanging on a wall in the living room, and she would put our names on the board and organize us into foot races. She drew lines in the dirt for the start line and a turnaround point where we would head back to the start line to finish the race. I guess it was a good way to keep us busy and out of trouble.

Sometimes Lolly, being a cheerleader, taught us how to do cartwheels, to run around, jump and cheer.

Manny also had plans for us. He would drag some mattresses into the living room, give us some boxing lessons and then organize the boxing rounds. It didn't last long after we got smart and started taking turns to fake a fall. That took the excitement out of boxing and soon Manny gave it up.

Some evenings, Mom and Dad would go visiting friends who had also moved from their villages to Fairbanks. They left us younger ones in the care of the older kids. We didn't like it when they left, and we cried and clung to Mom as if we were being abandoned and tortured.

One time, Irene told me to quit my crying and watch over Sugar and Tootie. I did, and was shocked at the craziness of their screaming, crying and carrying on. Tootie had to be held because she was ready to bolt out the door after Mom and Dad. When the car was backed out and heading up the road, she was released and I don't know quite how she did it, but she ran at top speed and stuck to the door! I saw what Irene was talking about and gave up that behavior myself. Tootie looked ridiculous!

When Birdie babysat, things got interesting because he always had plans. Sometimes, he would get us all pillows and hold pillow fights. It was fun, and when we hit the floor and started hollering in pain, he'd pick us up and assure us that we were fine. Then we'd go back to the fights. Mom tried to put a stop to the pillow fights when she realized what we were up to, because the corners of the pillowcases were wrinkled and took on the appearance of handles. We outsmarted her by ironing them before she and Dad returned home.

Birdie and Bing had some tricks up their sleeves, literally. They would ask us, "Want to see the moon?" Well of course I wanted to see the moon. They would instruct us, taking only one of us at a time out of sight of the others, to lie down on the floor. Then they'd take a coat, place it over that kid's face, tell her to look up a sleeve to the light. Then they'd pour water down the sleeve! No wonder they took us one at a time, telling each of us to not say a word, just watch the next one get fooled. And it was funny to see us fall victim to this trick time and time again. Great!

Other times, when Mom and Dad were gone, Birdie

organized a game where the couch in the living room was the "base." We all jumped onto the couch and Birdie would take a broom out. He would lift the broom and start swinging it up and down as one by one we took turns jumping off the couch and running under the swinging broom without getting hit. Then we'd run to the kitchen, around the dining table, back around the other side of the house, then back to the base. Once in a while, someone would get hit by the broom and the hollering and crying would stop everything. It never took Birdie long to convince the victim that they were going to be fine so that the game could continue.

It's funny, thinking back to those days. We had a television set, but I don't recall us sitting around watching it.

# NEW HOLIDAYS

We were familiar with Christmas and Easter holidays since they were part of our Catholic faith. At Holy Cross, everyone in the mission and most everyone in the village took part in the days that led up to midnight Mass of both celebrations. The church was decorated and there was baking. There were new dresses for us girls. The women dressed in their finest and the men and children were on their best behavior.

When we moved to Fairbanks, I became aware of new holidays and the different trappings that came with them. Holidays in Fairbanks were a whole new experience. Halloween was rather exciting. We learned about wearing masks and knocking on doors asking for candy. Since we lived way out of town and didn't really have neighbors, we had to go into town or find a neighborhood to work. In Fairbanks, there were two tall, huge apartment buildings. We figured the buildings were the way to go—we would be out of the cold and just go from door to door. So, we tried our luck. Right away, someone must have called the manager and we were back in the cold!

Mother's Day was a new one on us kids. It sounded good: a day for mothers. The only problem was, we didn't have any money to buy gifts or flowers.

Dad and Mom were both from the generation that didn't have pets. We had dogs, but they were for useful purposes such as hauling wood, going out to the trap line, traveling to Spring Camp, and of course racing. The dogs were not allowed in the house. And Mom wouldn't have anything to do with cats; she didn't trust them.

Sugar, Tootie and I learned about pet birds and creatures like turtles and little lizards. We tried talking Mom into getting us these interesting little pets but she was not interested in the least bit. So, in order to get around her, we waited and saved some money.

Finally, Mother's Day came around. We gathered our savings and went to Woolworths. Our first choice for her was a chameleon! It was so pretty, magically changing colors, and it was so slight of a creature. We brought it home and presented it to Mom. She was surprised when she opened the gift, and didn't know what to say or do but accept it. We had to tell her what it was, and that it could just hang out on her kitchen curtains. We said we would take care of it for her. She had no choice, so we killed two birds with one stone.

The little lizard lived for a while but then managed to fall into a crack in the wooden floor and we never saw it again. We felt so bad that we bought Mom a turtle!

# MOM'S WAY

Mom had her own way of dealing with us kids when we wanted her to do something special, like making "greasy pancakes" for us. I knew that when we were traveling on the boats there was no time to ask something special of her time. She was too busy cooking for the family and the crew. Everything was made from scratch and included homemade bread.

The greasy pancakes were sourdough pancakes, fried in lots of grease, making them crispy and delicious. They were a treat, not just restricted to breakfast. I remember asking Mom if she could make some, and she looked at me and said, "By and by."

I asked her when that was, and she simply replied, "By and by." I couldn't figure that one out; there was nothing specific about when that was to happen. With Christmas or a birthday, I knew when special treats would happen, but that "By and by" business seemed to just drift over time. When she was ready, she would make the requested thing happen.

Our chance to push the treat up came one summer when Dad, our brothers, and the crew made a quick trip, leaving Mom and us girls in Fairbanks. Without Dad and the boys, life seemed to slow down. Mom didn't have to follow the daily schedule that Dad needed to operate his business, so she must have taken advantage of a lighter workload. We slept in, ate when Mom cooked, and had the freedom to while away the days.

Summer days and nights in Fairbanks were normally hot, so Sugar, Tootie and I liked to take our small boat out onto the river, paddle around upriver, work our way back downriver, or paddle to the sandbar on the island across from our cabin. There we could wade in the shallow water, search for agates among the pebbles, or simply play all day.

Sugar, Tootie and I decided one day that we would trick Mom into making us greasy pancakes. The plan was to gather all of the ingredients and utensils she needed to make them, get everything down to the skiff and hide it away. Then we would invite Mom to go on a boat ride, which we didn't often do since her time was not usually her own.

She agreed, so we paddled her around for a while and then, when she was ready to go back to the house, we told her that we wanted greasy pancakes! I don't really know what she thought about that, but we brought out all the stuff and she agreed to do it. We built a fire by the river and she cooked. That was the day we managed to trick Mom past her "By and by" routine.

*Demientieff family and friends just back from a boat ride on the Chena.*

## "WHEN CROWS TURN WHITE"

The other phrase Mom used, when she wanted to put something off, was, "When the crows turn white!" During the winter months the only birds that flew about in the freezing cold were the ravens. There were no white seagulls in sight. They would return when the cold gave way to springtime and everything came back to life.

Finally, it was springtime and we were in Nenana on our first trip for the season. I was excited for the busy activities and the routine everyone knew had to happen. Dad had to do the grocery shopping for the trip, the crew was busy at work loading freight, and us kids had to stay out of the way. Mom would slip away to visit Auntie Dena for a while and we usually tagged along, knowing that Auntie Dena always had a pot of moose stew, homemade bread, or something else good to eat.

When we went back to the boats, I noticed the seagulls and got so excited. The crows had turned white. I raced over to tell Mom, "Look! The crows turned white!" and I pointed to the seagulls as they playfully flew about. She looked, and sure enough there they were. She must have been taken aback, but I reminded her that she had promised to make fish ice cream when the crows turned white. Mom was an expert at making this traditional treat.

# MOM, the CREATURE WHISPERER

One summer while walking in the woods with Mom, most likely looking for highbush cranberries, I heard a squirrel. At first it was a quick chirping, then as we made our way around, the squirrel's chirping got louder and longer.

I asked Mom what we were hearing and she was quiet, then looked at me and responded, "It's a squirrel." I wasn't satisfied so I asked her, "What is it saying?" She took her time but explained that the squirrel was warning the other creatures that human beings were in the forest.

I was so pleased with the idea that the squirrel was sending out warnings. Mom's words, "the creatures," "the forest," were so wonderful. They stirred my imagination and I kept this memory for a long time.

Time went by. Again, we were out in nature when suddenly I heard the quacking of ducks. Only it sounded like, "gluck, gluck, gluck." Again, I asked Mom what they were. She answered they were ducks. I was expecting another wonderful interpretation, so again I asked her what they were saying. With a smile and a sparkle in her eyes she simply said, "Gluck Gluck!"

# BACK ON THE RIVER: FAIRBANKS TO HOLY CROSS

*Demientieff family on the* Sea Wolf *at their Chena River Landing. Manny, not in photo, was serving in the military.*

*Launching the big Demientieff barge from the skids at their Chena River landing.*

# RIVER REFLECTIONS

While writing these stories of my childhood and thinking about traveling the rivers with my dad and mom, brothers and sisters, I remembered moments as a child where I had questioning thoughts. These were thoughts that I didn't understand, and I felt I had no one to talk to about. As I write about the experiences I had as an older child, I remember having more of these reflective moments. The following memory is of the summer we left Fairbanks to return to Holy Cross and the mission.

The ice and snow had melted away, vanished as though winter had never happened. With spring in full bloom, Mom and Dad were instructing us kids in preparations to get our trip underway. Our home in Fairbanks was emptied of pots, pans, dishes, silverware, blankets, pillows and our personal items, all carried to the boats. We were going back to Holy Cross!

After we were all on board and the men untied the outfit,

Dad would skillfully take the boats and barge out and slowly turn it all around. The Chena River is not very wide, so this was always something to watch.

As the boat moved along the river, away from our cabin in Fairbanks, I was starting to appreciate our life on the river and to feel free of everything that tied us to the city. After living in the city, and with another year behind me, I felt changes within me. I was becoming more aware of life around me and how we were all changing.

It didn't take us long traveling on the peaceful Chena River to reach the Tanana River, which is a much larger, wider and swifter river. The clear water of the Chena mixed with the muddier waters of the Tanana and then disappeared into its murky depths. Because the Tanana currents were stronger, now and then I'd notice the swirling waters of an eddy and enjoy its mesmerizing effect.

Where the Chena poured into the Tanana, Dad had to speed up the boats as we entered the stronger currents. Once he cleared the riverbanks, he would swing the barge around and head us downriver to another summer of adventure.

*Riverboat and barge at the Nenana railroad dock.*

# NENANA

Our first stop this trip was Nenana, which is at a crossroads of the highway and the railroad that both connect to Anchorage. Nenana is a major port for moving freight in and out of Interior Alaska. It was not like the other villages we traveled to; it was so busy and exciting.

The docks along the river were busy with tug boats all working with the barges that were loading and unloading cargo. There was the *Taku Chief*, which both Uncle Alphonse and Uncle Tony worked on, and there were the railroad boats, the steamers *Nenana* and *Alice*. Dad and Mom were the only boat with kids aboard. All of the others had men as their deckhands.

Once the boats were tied off and the plank connected us to the docks, Dad would head to Coghill's store, followed by Sugar, Tootie, and me, running to keep up with him. At the store, the owner was always glad to see Dad coming because we bought our food supplies there, by the case.

Dad was very good at math. He kept an eye on everything he bought, and when he was given the total, he could always catch a mistake. When Dad paid for everything, he merely said, "Charge it. Charge it to Nick E. Demientieff." Then he would sign the paper and all was done. Sugar, Tootie, and I decided to try that out one time. We shopped for candy and when we made our selection, we simply told Bob, "Charge it. Charge it to Nick E. Demientieff." We got away with it!

Nenana was also home to Dad's older brother and his wife, Uncle Alphonse and Auntie Mary, and Dad's sister, Auntie Dena, and her husband, Uncle Tony. So, we had cousins to visit and play with. While Dad and the crew worked at loading the freight, Mom and us kids would walk past tall cottonwood trees on a nice little path leading us to Auntie Dena's house. She always had a pot of moose soup or something tasty to eat.

There was a huge black railroad bridge over the Tanana River, and across the river from the community were the Nenana hills. The hills were covered with white birch trees with dancing green leaves. About a third of the way up the hill there was a large white cross standing over a graveyard, with little white fences that seemed to be guarding each grave.

*The Alaska Railroad trestle and depot at Nenana. The bridge was built in 1923.*

## "THE RIVER OPENS WIDE"

With the freight loaded onto our barges, Dad and the crew worked quickly at getting us back onto the river. There is a big bend just below Nenana, and, once beyond the bend, the river opens wide like a big welcome.

After all the flurry, everyone was now able to relax. Dad retreated to the pilothouse where he was able to look over the load of freight, check the flag for wind direction, and study the river. The engine ran constantly; the subtle vibration of the boat was easy to get used to again.

I decided to get away from it all and made my way to the front of the barge. I climbed over the freight to find a spot to nestle in and watch the landscape slowly change. Out on the barge there was calm, peace and quiet. I relaxed and took in the moment, the fresh air, cool breeze and solitude. It was a perfect time to let my mind wander. My thoughts drifted to Holy Cross, our house, the village and the Mission. I was wondering was it still the same?

The rivers themselves fascinated me with their constant movement, flowing sometimes swiftly, sometimes calm. Even the colors of the rivers changed.

This trip, we stayed on the Tanana River until we reached the town of Tanana, where our boat moved into the Yukon River. Our next stops were Ruby, Galena and Holy Cross, places that were most likely to have freight for delivery.

We stopped at the village of Ruby, where Uncle Alfred and Auntie Marianne Gurtler lived with their big family. They were very close to Mom and Dad—the four had shared a double wedding ceremony in 1929. Dad maneuvered the *Sea Wolf* in for landing and the men secured the boats.

To get ashore, Sugar, Tootie and I walked on the plank behind Mom and were then free to run about. The kids of Ruby were usually friendly, but for some reason on this visit, some of them were more challenging. They taunted us, saying things like, "You're not Native!"

This was upsetting, so we ran to Birdie and Bing so they could come to our rescue. They were not afraid to defend us and would put up their fists and say, "Come on, put up yer dukes!" The bullies backed down and ran off!

I wondered why those kids would say something like that. When I looked at myself in the mirror, I saw a girl with hazel eyes and long brown hair, always braided when we stopped at a village. I thought I was rather normal looking. With the words, "You're not Native," I started to question what it was that made them say that.

What is it that makes a person Native? I realized then that we didn't speak our Native language and I wondered why. It was one of the thoughts that bothered me. I simply blamed Mom and Dad!

Finally, we landed at Holy Cross and it was great to be back home. I couldn't wait to get to our house, run up the stairs and look out the two upstairs windows at each end of the house. From one window I could see that the Mission, the gardens and the church were still there, and from the other window I could see that all the houses and the sand bar were there as well.

It was exciting and fun to be back with our friends. They were interested in learning about Fairbanks, but I was more interested in what was happening in the village.

# HOLY CROSS MISSION SCHOOL, 1952

*An early photo of the Holy Cross Mission buildings. Photo courtesy Alaska State Library.*

# BOARDING at HOLY CROSS MISSION

In 1952, when I was seven, Mom and Dad placed Birdie, Bing, Joanne, Irene and me in the Holy Cross Mission boarding school for about three weeks. If I recall correctly, they only did this when they had to deliver freight farther down the Yukon River where the waters were closer to the Bering Sea and the boat voyage was too treacherous for us kids.

Our mission stay was quite the experience since we had never stayed overnight at the Catholic mission. As village kids, we had shared a classroom with the mission kids during the school day but hadn't socialized with them much or known what it was like to live in a dorm all the time. That was the first and only time it happened and that experience had an impact on my life!

*Holy Cross Mission. Sisters' House visible to right of church, Jesuit House to the left, and large cross on hill to right.*

## The MISSION BUILDINGS

The mission had a church with a front door that faced the river, a tower with a large bell, and a pathway lined with a row of birch trees. There was a small hospital, a residence for the Sisters, one for the Fathers, and dorm rooms for children of all ages who came from all across Alaska. There was a girls' playground and a boys' playground, each with swings, a seesaw, and a tall metal pole with chains that hung down so we could grab them and run in a circle until our speed lifted us into the air.

## The SISTERS of SAINT ANN

Life in the mission was very different from living with Mom, Dad, my brothers and sisters. I didn't know what to make of the Sisters. They were religious women who had taken vows to serve God by going wherever they were needed.

Everything they wore was black except the oval-shaped white starched material that framed their faces. Black veils were attached somehow to these white frames and continued over the top of their heads and streamed down over their shoulders. Each Sister wore a skirt with many layers, a shirt, a vest and high-top shoes with laces. Wooden beads linked with a gold chain were attached to a belt that swung freely as she moved about. The beads made a jangling sound that announced the nuns' comings and goings.

They were very serious and spoke with authority. In my first encounters, I don't recall any of them smiling. At first, I was afraid of the Sisters, dressed all in black, covered from head to toe—not a sign of skin or hair to indicate that they were human.

*Holy Cross Mission School.*

# BOARDING SCHOOL LIFE

Birdie and Bing had to stay in the boys' dorm. Irene and Lumpy were placed in the big girls' dorm on the third floor, and I stayed with the little girls on the second floor. I think this was the first time that we were ever separated as a family.

We little girls had our own area with all the little beds in rows, one long sink with a row of faucets for running water, and an area enclosed by curtains for potty chambers. When I met the other little girls, I was comforted. I remember Margie, Gloria, Cecilia, Mary, and Eileen especially, and there were others I enjoyed playing and spending time with.

Although our stay in the mission was brief, I remember discovering how life for the children at the mission was very different than my life with my family. And since we were in the mission such a short time, we were not subjected to every rule the mission kids had to follow. For example, all the little girls' hair was cut short at the mission, while my hair was long and usually in braids. I remember Dad telling the Sisters not to cut our hair.

I thought of the mission girls as my playmates, playmates that I lived with. The village kids had parents and went home from school every night.

Our times together were governed by the activities of the day, mostly praying. The morning routine started with Sister Mary Alice waking us up. When we rose to meet the day, we got on our knees, hands folded, our eyes closed and head tilted downward. As we prayed, I always peeked to see if I was doing the right thing. After morning prayer, we washed our faces, brushed our teeth, combed our hair, and got dressed for the day, all in silence.

Then we made our way to the dining room in single file, still in silence. The dining room was huge with tables and benches awaiting our presence. The boys joined us for meals but didn't sit with the girls. We took our places at the tables and after the food was on our trays, we again said a prayer in thanksgiving. After that, one of the Sisters would indicate that we were free to eat.

After all the silence, and given the number of kids in the room, it was impressive to hear the chattering and clanging of the forks and spoons against the metal trays. That really started the day. After our meal, we prayed again before we returned to our daily chores and activities.

*Some of the older mission girls worked with the Sisters in the Holy Cross mission kitchen. This photo is from the 1930s (Photo from Sisters of St. Ann archives).*

# CHORES

Since I was a little girl, my chores were not very demanding. I liked to go to the dispensary. The room had its own distinct smells. There was an assortment of medicines—pills, and liquids such as cod liver oil. I imagined both the health and sickness there. I went there because I liked Sister Mary Edward who gave out the medications. She had a twinkle in her eye and was friendly and kind. She spoke with a little accent. She wore a long, dark blue bib-style apron.

Sister Mary Edward dispensed medications to the mission students and staff, and also had time set aside for the village people. Every day one of us little girls was to walk about the halls ringing a hand bell. This was a signal that it was time for mission kids to get their medications. I liked ringing that hand bell. It was not that often I had the chance, so when I did get to ring the bell, I took it quite seriously. Perhaps that was the first time I thought of myself as a mission kid and not a village kid.

One of our other chores was to climb the stairs to the top floor of the Sisters' building. There were windows all along the room and rows of pews, like a chapel. This was where we went to mend socks—the boys' socks! It was very tedious work, threading a mending needle and then stretching a single sock over a wooden form to hold it in place for the mending process. After chores, we had time to play outdoors.

One time I went with Addie, one of the bigger girls, to do her chores. I thought she was beautiful. She worked quietly and I helped her fold sheets and other linens up on the top floor of the four-story dorm building.

It was dark as we climbed up the wooden stairs, but when we reached the fourth floor it was a wide-open space. There were no rooms, just an open area with storage cabinets where the folded linens were stored. There were windows all along the walls that faced the Yukon River and overlooked the village. I was so impressed at how much one could see of the river from this room.

# SUNDAYS at the MISSION

On Sunday, we had to go to Mass. The regular mission kids wore their uniforms, but I just used my own clothes. We filed into the church, just like what I witnessed as a village kid, only this time I was up front with the mission kids. Up close, I watched the priest go through the motions of the Mass. There were small booklets for us to use, where the service was all written out, one side in English and the other in Latin. I worked to keep up. Being in the front, I didn't have time to daydream or stare off at the artwork. I had to participate! I loved the songs and prayers that were in Latin.

*Children on the mission boat,* Little Flower, *perhaps on their way to go berry picking.*

## PICNIC in the MEADOW

Now and then during our stay in the mission, we were taken for a picnic in the meadow. It was quite a big event. Sister Mary Ida, Sister Mary Jude, the priests and Brothers, all worked together to load up the truck with food and supplies for the day.

Once there, the big kids helped the Sisters and priests start a fire and prepare the food. We all had jackets and scarves for our walk together down the dirt road to the meadow, past our family's house and the village and along the river. Trees fringed both sides of this huge, open clearing, full of long grasses, flowers and frogs. I found the meadow magical, perfect for games and fun, with fresh air and the freedom to run and play.

After the day was over, the old truck was again loaded with tired, sleepy kids to return to the Mission, with its strict routine and the musky smells. I learned that the movie star, Bing Crosby, had donated the truck we rode in, and later, when I saw him in his movies, I could make the connection. I would wonder about that truck and how in the heck did a movie star hear about Holy Cross?

# SISTER MARY ALICE and the MUCKINJACKS

Sister Mary Alice was responsible for the little girls of the mission. She was small in stature and spoke with a foreign accent, but she was kind and friendly.

One hot sunny day, Sister Mary Alice took us little girls for a swim in the Yukon River. We walked up the dusty road from the mission buildings and out to the river. We slipped out of our towels and waded into the silty, greyish, chilly river. At first it was cold and we tiptoed along the shallow areas. Then some of the girls got brave and into the water they went. I finally got brave and, once in, I forgot about the coldness of the water. I started playing, splashing and jumping up and down. I don't know how long we played, but when Sister Mary Alice started calling to us to come out of the water, no one listened, even though she called and called.

It must have been frustrating for her because she couldn't come in after us, with all her skirts, beads and her high, black-laced shoes. All she could do was walk back and forth along the river. Finally, she hollered, "Hurry up, get out of the water and be careful—be careful of the muckinjacks!"

Sister Mary Alice never raised her voice, so to hear her hollering something about "muckinjacks" got our attention. We all started running, quickly making our way out of the river and onto the shore. I never saw a bunch of little girls move so fast. But just the thought of a muckinjack, whatever that was, was terrifying! Years later, I still recall that day when little Sister Mary Alice found a way to get us out of the river!

# The MOVIE HALL

The movie hall was actually a Quonset hut on a concrete foundation, located on the mission grounds. Every Sunday, most everyone from the village and the mission filed into the building for a movie. Inside was basically the same setup as the church, with wooden benches in two rows. One side was for the girls and the other for the boys, with an aisle down the middle. There was a huge screen in the front of the room, a large film projector in the middle. Behind the projector there were more benches, with the last row raised up like a bleacher seat.

The first film was always the newsreel, showing events that took place somewhere out in the world—baseball, football, war news and other things. Then there was the news of Hollywood, and a quick peek at the movie stars who would be up on the screen, too. Finally, we saw the anticipated film. The first huge reel of film was placed upon the projector and, with a clicking sound, the movie started. We never knew what we were going to see but that didn't matter. There was the musical opening and an announcer heralding the movie's title and its stars, like Clark Gable. The girls would swoon at each mention of the name of a star. Every movie introduced us to a hero, to villains, beautiful women and handsome men and a few kids. I was transported into each of those stories, identifying with whomever I chose.

There were two films every Sunday night. When the movies were over, everyone would make their way home, either to the village or the Mission. After one of these movie nights, when we were living in the Mission, a few of us were making our way back to the dorm when we ducked into the Sisters' building on the first floor, where it was dark and quiet.

The film we had just seen must have been a scary one or a story about a mischievous kid. I just remember I had decided to be that mischievous kid.

I walked along the wooden floor and made my way to the

long hallway leading to the door to the long row of outhouses outside. The hallway had a coat rack that ran the length of the hall, and beneath the coats were bins for shoes. I climbed onto a bin and hid behind the coats. There was a single bare lightbulb hanging from the ceiling, with a long chain to switch it on and off. The light was on, but it was quite dim.

My intention was to jump out and scream to scare the living daylights out of my chosen victim. I waited, let a couple of kids go by, and then made up my mind—this is it; the next one gets it! Little did I know that it would be one of the Sisters.

I was a little girl, but had the advantage of standing on the bin, which would place me at about the same level as an adult. I jumped out screaming, and was stunned to see Sister Mary Ida. I don't remember what happened next.

# LONESOME DAYS

Sometimes I'd get lonesome, so I'd go to the big girls' side to be with Irene and Lumpy. There I got to know some of the other big girls. Among them were Addie, Pauline, Della Mae, Laura, Emily, and others.

After I got used to the strict routine at the mission, I started to appreciate Mom, Dad, our family, and our home very much. I began to get homesick. I would cry to Irene, and she did her best to reassure me that Mom and Dad would be coming back soon.

Days went by and my sadness grew. I remembered the big room upstairs, and climbed the stairs. No one was there, so I went to look out the windows like I would at home. The Sisters' building was three stories high, so I could see a greater distance. I looked over the village, our house, Grandma's house—everything was there. When I saw the Yukon River, I let my eyes follow it downriver to the point of the bend. I could see the trees, one leaning over like it could fall into the river at any moment.

I was waiting to see the front of our barge coming around that bend, with the white flag blowing in the wind. I waited for what seemed like hours before I realized that it was not going to happen that day. I would cry there all by myself.

At last, Dad came for us, and I was so relieved. I would never want to be separated from them again. Birdie, Bing, Lumpy, Irene, and I went home!

Many years later when I remembered those lonely moments, I realized that I had always had Mom and Dad, and they always came to get us to return to our home. But I wondered about what had happened to my little buddies and the rest of the mission kids. When would they get to go home?

# FIRST FLIGHT

That fall, Dad was taking more time than usual in returning us to Fairbanks. Irene, Sugar and I were enrolled in public school in Fairbanks and we were going to miss the first days of school if we went back by boat. Dad decided to send us back to Fairbanks by plane. I had seen other people travel that way but this would be the first time for me.

Up to that point, the planes that I had seen all had wheels and landed on sandbars. This plane was bigger and landed on the river. Dad always called floatplanes "pontoon ships."

We were all dressed for the trip and had our suitcases with us. We climbed into the plane and the engines started. The plane was sitting low in the water, the pilot revved up the engines, the plane lifted a bit and slowly started moving forward. The skies were cloudy and gray, and the wind was blowing hard enough to whip up white caps on the river. I wasn't sure about this, but what could I do?

*"Pontoon ships" on the river at Holy Cross, 1940s. The floatplane on the left is a five-passenger Gullwing Stinson.*

The engines growled and we continued moving forward, hitting the waves, with river water splashing on the windows and up and over the plane. I was scared, remembering what I'd seen in the movies. I thought, "We're in a submarine, we're going under!" I closed my eyes as if that would make it all go away, but soon we lifted off into the sky. Once up, we flew over the village, the meadow, and the mission.

We flew to Lake Minchumina Airport, a place that I never heard of, and when we got out of the plane, I asked Irene where we were and where we were going. I had too many questions and I needed answers! She reassured me that we were going to Fairbanks. I wasn't convinced, thinking that she, too, must have doubts.

At Lake Minchumina Airport, we switched to a plane on wheels and then continued on to McGrath, then Anchorage, and lastly to Fairbanks. The plane must have had other stops to make that complicated its route. It was a long trip. Beforehand, I didn't know that we had so many stops along the way, so I grew more doubtful. Each stop I would ask again, "Where are we?" I think with my growing doubts and fears, I was beginning to plant thoughts of worry and concern in Irene as well. Finally, we landed in Fairbanks!

# COPPER VALLEY SCHOOL, 1958 TO 1964

Copper Valley School was operated by the Catholic church from 1956 to 1971. The school was known for high academic standards, and at its peak gathered a statewide student body of more than 150 students. The school's buildings were destroyed by fire in 1976.

# The BEGINNINGS of CVS

The existence of Copper Valley School (CVS) goes back to Holy Cross and the dream of some Jesuits and the Sisters of St. Ann to establish the Catholic Church and mission schools for the Native people of Alaska. When the Holy Cross Mission was closed, the remaining Sisters and students there moved to CVS, continuing this thread of service.

The new school was a boarding school with an emphasis on building leadership in the students. It was fueled by prayer, donations, volunteers, time and talent. Students came from villages from the north and west and along the Yukon and Tanana Rivers and from Southwest Alaska.

When Father Fallert, the principal, came to visit Mom and Dad, Irene, Sam and Joanne were already attending CVS and I was ready to go, too.

# MY FIRST YEAR at COPPER, 7th GRADE

My first year at the school was both exciting and a little scary. It was the first time I heard of kids being homesick. For me, at 12, it was hard to be away from home, from Mom, Dad, and my little sisters, Sugar and Tootie.

The school was still under construction, so temporary classrooms were set up wherever they could fit. The sleeping quarters for the girls was one big dorm room filled with metal, military-style beds with springs and thin mattresses, all neatly arranged. My sister Irene's bed was next to mine, but my bed was the last in the long row, right next to an outer door, which I didn't like. But I had Irene there to watch over me. At some point during the night at least one of us girls cried—cried for home, our parents and friends. It was a soft, sad sound and swept like a wave through the dorm.

The bigger girls took care of the little girls, comforting and assuring us that everything was going to be all right.

# The CLASSROOM

During seventh grade, our classroom was on the ground level of a two-story structure. Desks were set up between a private room/office and the girls' bathroom/shower area. A blackboard was attached to the wall and our little desks were in rows. There was also a huge desk for our teacher, Sister Denise Marie, a tall, thin nun with hard-rimmed glasses, a serious face, and stern looks.

My desk was in the front row on the left of the room, and my friend Eileen's desk was on the opposite side. Hers was the last in her row. Eileen and I met earlier in the Holy Cross Mission school where she was a mission kid and I was a village kid. We were the smallest among the girls, so when there was a shortage of books, we sat together, sharing books and secrets.

There was an open hallway that led past the girls' bathroom, connecting to the second makeshift classroom, which was for eighth-graders. There were more boys in that group, and a young boy named Donny caught my eye.

One day I was instructed to go to Eileen's desk to share a book and I was happy to do that. As our teacher, Sister Denise Marie, was writing on the blackboard, Eileen and I peeked from behind our book to get a good look at Donny in the next room. While we sat whispering back and forth, I realized that Sister had stopped talking. We froze, then turned back just in time to see an eraser fly between our heads. Shoooosh—she missed! Then I was ordered back to my desk. From that moment on, I realized I had to keep an eye on the teacher.

Our small row consisted of me, Mary, another girl, and our one boy, Michael. At some point we got together and decided that if Sister was to throw an eraser at me, all I had to do was duck, and then Mary, the other girl, and then Michael would have to duck, too.

The day came, and as Sister Denise Marie took aim at me, I ducked. Mary ducked, the other girl ducked, but Michael was sitting at his desk daydreaming. That eraser caught his attention but it didn't seem to faze him. The rest of us got good at avoiding the little missiles, but Michael didn't even bother. Michael was so smart that all he had to do was to look through a book and he'd understand the material. I had to work hard trying to grasp some of it.

One day the assignment was to write a short story and be prepared to read it in front of the class. When the time came for the reading of our stories, Sister called out my name—I was the first one. I was so scared. I grabbed my single sheet of paper and stood before the class, trying to hide behind my paper and hide my fear.

At first my voice was meek, shaky and not loud enough to be understood. Sister Denise Marie, in her loud booming voice, instructed me to speak louder. I tried my hardest, but it wasn't enough, and she bellowed out again at me to be louder.

I couldn't take it. I burst into tears and ran to the bathroom to hide away. I don't remember if it was her booming voice that triggered my tears, but the other kids fell silent. I was within hearing distance, hanging onto one of the sinks, when I recognized Mary's voice speaking up, asking our teacher in a strong demanding tone why she had yelled at me. I was stunned that someone had stood up for me. I don't recall if there was any answer, but Mary's question gave me the courage to return to the front of the class and carry on as if nothing had happened.

One day Sister Denise Marie called me aside and explained that she had taught my brothers and sisters in the past, but they had been older then than I was now. I had come along and was younger, and she said she was going to break my spirit. I didn't know what that meant, but the seriousness of her voice made me determined not to trust her again. I kept that little secret to myself, but I paid close attention to her from then on.

# DANCE INSTRUCTION

Sister Denise Marie was not only my teacher by day, she was the dance instructor for all of the students for our regular lessons. She taught us the Tango, Fox Trot, ball room dancing, waltzing, and square dancing. I enjoyed dancing, so I relished every moment of that class.

Sister Denise was an excellent dancer and a good instructor. She didn't let a thing slip from her attention. As the dance form we were learning changed, she paired us up with new partners. Then she gave us the freedom to dance with whomever we wanted. One of the boys came up to me, bowed his head, and asked me for the next dance. I simply looked past him and rejected his very nice offer. I was a little brat; I was looking about, hoping someone else would come to my rescue.

Before that could happen, though, Sister came right over to us, and, taking advantage of this teachable moment, she said, "You never reject an invitation. You just accept it." My lesson for the day was that the boy and I were to be partners for the rest of the year!

*Tiny on snowshoes at Copper Valley School.*

# The BANQUET

As the school year clicked by, so did the usual seasonal events like Christmas, Easter, and our birthdays. For each holiday there was a different experience. Sometimes we had a banquet where we dressed up: the girls wore nice dresses and the boys wore their white shirts and ties. The tables were all dressed up with linen, silverware, and glasses. There were real dishes, not the usual metal military trays. It was all first class.

There was one banquet where I was being recognized for something and I was sitting up front at the table of honor. As a beautiful meal was set before us, I was thrilled with each course, every dish that passed in front of me—and, of course, dessert. In keeping with the dress code, I was wearing a dress and high heels. The high heels were not that comfortable, so I used my feet to play with them under the table. What I didn't know was that the tablecloths were short and didn't reach the floor.

So, while I was eating and enjoying myself, others could see that my feet were busy chasing and searching for my shoes. Sister Mary Alice came to me and whispered, "Tiny, you might want to sit up and behave yourself. The tablecloths are short and the kids are watching and laughing at you."

I shot up in my chair with big eyes, and immediately corrected my posture and my behavior for the rest of the evening!

*Teenage Tiny, CVS years.*

# WEEKENDS

Each and every weekend was special to us. Once we had completed our work week and it was Saturday, we were assigned the next round of chores. Saturday was also the day we could wear jeans. Every Saturday night something was happening—a dance, a talent show, games night, and on and on. I think we had a great social life but since there was no dating, we all got together for fun.

*Left to right: Sister Kathleen Mary, Sister Mary Ida ("Smida"), Sister Mary Alice Therese, Sister Christine Marie, Sister Mary Ann Rita, Sister Mary Eulalia, Sister Mary George Edmund (superior). From Ron Kunkel Collection, Copper Valley School Association Archives.*

Sundays started off with the Mass and we had to wear dresses, but after breakfast, we were free to do whatever we wanted until suppertime.

Some walked to "Brenwicks," the little store next to the highway. Some snuck off to the tulies for a smoke, some hiked around, and some just stretched out for a good long nap. After supper, we had free time again before the movie. One of the staff volunteers ran our little school store, "the Canteen," and stocked it with candy, pop, and snacks. The ending of the movie signaled the end of the weekend, and back to routine.

# SMIDA—SISTER MARY IDA

Sister Mary Ida was a tall, thin Sister of the Congregation of the Sisters of Saint Ann. She was a nun from Canada. Because like all nuns she was not married and had no kids, I never saw her as a woman, at least not like any woman I ever met. She wore veils, a starched head-dress, long black-laced shoes and jangling beads. She was the cook for the school and ruled the kitchen with an iron fist.

One day, something I did set her off and she was on fire. I didn't wait around for an explanation. I just took off running with her on my tail, her veils and beads swinging. I ran from the kitchen, making my way through the long dining hall and out the huge door. I glanced over my shoulder and she, with her long legs, was making good time and closing in on me.

I ran around the school circle and as I was coming to the chapel, I had a bright idea. She wouldn't dare do anything to me in front of God. I slowed myself and entered the chapel in a respectful and reverent manner. Walking slowly up to the communion rail, I knelt down, crossed myself and started praying.

Out of curiosity, I glanced back and there she was, pacing back and forth in front of the doors. She didn't set a foot into God's house and I returned to my prayerful pose. I got caught up in prayer and only gradually remembered I was hiding out from an upset "Smida." I carefully walked to the chapel doors and glanced around. She was nowhere in sight—she was gone!

To this day, I don't remember what I did to trigger the moment that set her off, but I fondly remember the safety of God's house.

# The PANTRY

One quiet Saturday afternoon, I decided to help out in the kitchen. I made my way to Smida and volunteered to clean the pantry. She was surprised and pleased. She gave me an apron, and walked me to the pantry. Always very dramatic, she waved her arms to explain what she wanted done. I was to move the row of huge tin storage cans, sweep the floor, and give it all a general cleaning.

I got busy moving the cans, remembering how the crew from the barge moved gas drums, by grabbing the side of a can and carefully guiding it by rolling it along. So proud of myself, I got things ready to sweep the floor.

First, though, I decided to check out what was in the cans. There were basic things like sugar, flour, and other stuff, but one of the tins contained loose candy that smelled wonderful. It was like Christmas and I couldn't resist. I filled my apron pocket, considering that after all, the candy was a reward for volunteering.

After I finished the cleaning, I proudly informed Smida that my work was finished. I don't know what I thought she would give me, but I was pleased that I had already found my reward. She smiled, put her arm around me and we turned to go to the pantry.

To my horror, as we walked slowly along, we were following a trail of candy. I felt myself shrinking inside, but not one word was spoken. When we got to the pantry, I froze. She turned to me and calmly said, "You know, you didn't have to steal. I would have given you the candy." My days of stealing didn't end, but this event did slow me down!

*Sister Mary Ida, in charge of the CVS kitchen, procured food and supplies on a small budget and from donations. She "had skinning races with...returning hunters," says Margaret Cantwell in her book* North to Share: Sisters of Saint Ann in Alaska and the Yukon Territory. *When CVS ran out of onions, this truck arrived as an answer to prayer, with 50 bushels of onions sent by a California friend of the school.*

## The FATHERS' DINING ROOM

I was assigned for one week to work in the Fathers' dining room, which meant cleaning up after meals, sweeping the floor, and making sure things were in their proper places and free of dust. On Saturday, I had to do deep cleaning, which meant removing all of the condiment jars, wiping them down, and returning them to the cabinet where they were stored.

I was wiping the various jars when I came across one filled with what looked like peanut butter. We only got that savory stuff on Sundays, but I thought, why not as a Saturday reward? I quickly grabbed a tablespoon, not a teaspoon, and spooned a generous portion from the jar into my salivating mouth. I was anticipating bliss but Heaven was short lived. As soon as I closed my lips to make sure I got every little bit of it, my eyes started watering and my mouth was on fire. I ran to the bathroom, just off the kitchen, as fast as I could go—to get rid of whatever was in my mouth. I finally got the stuff out, but the bitterness lingered.

Back at the scene of the crime, I took a good look at the jar and realized it was labeled "Horseradish."

## BASKETBALL

Basketball was the main game at Copper Valley and we loved it. We devoted winter nights and weekends to basketball, and when the official season was over, we put together more games.

Sometimes it was staff against students, sometimes the men versus the women. During this one particular game, it was the female staff playing against the girls. The staff had the advantage of being taller, older, and one would think more experienced. What I didn't realize at the time was that we were younger and had all of the advantages of training in the game.

*Tiny, front left, cheerleader at CVS. Photo from* Scuttlebutt, *the school newsletter. Photo courtesy Copper Valley School Association Archives.*

Smida started off as the staff center since she was the tallest one in the house. The tip off happened and the game started. We hustled back and forth, playing with furious determination. The game must have been close, because the gym was quiet and we were all fighting hard. Then all of a sudden, the ball disappeared.

The hollering stopped and we all looked around for the ball. Smida was playing ball in her nun's habit, skirts, veils and head dress, and I realized the ball must be under her skirts, but I was not going to find out. The disappearance of the ball even stunned Smida, until she gathered her thoughts and reached under her skirts—and out came the ball.

# DECEMBER

December had its own routine. The school was decorated every year with a Christmas wreath that hung in the dining room—the Advent wreath. I think the wreath was something that all the Sisters had a hand in preparing. Each wreath was rather big, made of spruce branches that were shaped and formed into a circle that lay flat.

*Teenage Tiny with Santa Claus at Copper Valley School.*

Four big candles were set within the wreath to represent the four weeks of the month. The first three candles were white and the last was pink. Each Sunday, the candles were lit and prayers were recited as part of the Advent service.

The month of December had a two-week holiday, a break for those who could take advantage of that time to return home. The kids that came from the outlying villages generally remained at the school and had their own little Christmas with the staff.

# A DEATH in the FAMILY

In December, 1958, my older brother, Birdie, my sisters Lumpy, Irene, and I all went back to our Fairbanks home for Christmas.

Winter in the Interior was very cold, but our big cabin was warm, cozy, and welcoming. We were all busy helping with cleaning, getting the house ready for the tree, decorations, and Christmas. Temperatures had dipped down into the minus, 40 to 50 below zero.

It was a common event to witness the northern lights as they danced magically across the sky. The colors of the flashing lights moved constantly, shifting and changing. The cold was accompanied with glistening snow, which reflected bright moonlight and stars. It was easy to locate the Big Dipper, the Little Dipper, and the North Star when the stars twinkled, but the bitter sharp cold made me move just as quickly back into the warmth of the house.

Manny, our eldest brother, was an adult by then and Dad had helped him realize his dream of flying airplanes. Once he learned how to fly and got his private license, he then had his own airplane. Our cousins, Florence (Bubbles) and Bernice, had come home from CVS with us and it was planned that Manny would fly them to Ruby, so they could spend the holiday at their home.

I remember it as if it were yesterday. After the darkness of the winter morning gave way to sunny skies, Manny warmed up his airplane on the frozen Chena River, right in front of the house. Bubbles and Bernice gathered their things for the flight home. They all climbed aboard, taxied out, lifted off, and disappeared from sight.

A day or two passed and Manny had not yet returned from his trip. We were all busy shopping and getting last minute things done.

I do remember that Mom and Dad were worried, and then there was a knock at the door. Manny was missing. I don't remember if we, Birdie, Lumpy, Irene, and I were whisked away, back to the school. I don't remember if we had Christmas at the house, but it was all over. The wreckage of the airplane was located and Manny was gone.

I was confused and angry. I didn't know what was going on, but here we were back on schedule as if nothing happened. Something deep within me changed. I was agitated, frustrated, and didn't know who or what to blame. Perhaps it was then that I started to stuff my secrets away, thinking perhaps they would just disappear.

When I was younger, I always ran to Irene for answers and help, but since now I was "older," I must have been testing myself again and seeing what I could hide or forget. I knew for sure that Manny was gone, but I didn't know what happened. His death was the first loss that our family had to face.

I'm not sure how Mom and Dad lived through it, and I know that they, too, were lost for a long time. I tried to talk to Mom about Manny, but her demeanor would instantly change. At first it was pain, then she stiffened up, as if to brace herself, and she'd firmly tell me that we would not talk of it anymore. My questions about Manny had to wait until I was older, much older.

*Manny in Holy Cross. His death in 1958 was very difficult for Tiny and her family.*

One evening when it was time for study hall, I was the first to arrive in the classroom. I found my desk and plopped down. I've since learned that sometimes it's not good to think too much or for too long about a painful situation like death. But that is what happened that night; I felt my agitation and frustration coming up and it quickly turned to anger. I looked around at what I could do with it, and as I scanned the room, I noticed a tack. I put it on the teacher's chair and, in that moment, I thought it was a masterful move.

Kids started filling the room and I sat there, so smug. Then Sister Mary Anne Evelyn came strolling through the door. I realized I hadn't planned on her being the one to sit down on the tack, but there was nothing I could do about it, so I sat down and kept an eye on her. She was happily chatting about her dad's bakery and all the goodies she enjoyed as a child. She was a chubby one.

Finally, she sat down, but nothing happened. I didn't understand why—she should have jumped right back out of the chair, but she simply sat down, opened a book, and settled down for the hour-long period of silence. I sat there and tried to figure out what went wrong. I figured that one of two things happened: she either hit the crack of her seat right on the tack, or, because she was wearing so many veils and stuff the tack never touched her.

I later wondered if maybe this little act of mine released some of my pent-up anger. Thank goodness she didn't become a victim of my actions.

# MY SECOND YEAR at COPPER, 8th GRADE

Summer months at Copper Valley School were busy with construction. The school buildings were slowly but surely coming together. Volunteers worked hard and gave months of their lives and personal time to make the dream of the school a reality.

Once August was fading, it was time to get back to the school for another year of growing, learning, and getting to know each other on a deeper level. Buses were sent to both Fairbanks and Anchorage to pick up Copper students arriving from throughout Alaska. I was traveling by bus from Fairbanks with a lively bunch of kids, some familiar and some new.

Our girls' dorm was in the building next to the Infirmary. The ground level was dedicated to the little girls. There was a private room for the girls' Prefect, a bathroom, showers, two tubs, an ironing area, and a huge laundry sink.

The upper level, we called it "Heaven," had rooms for the big girls and the same basic floor plan. Sister Mary Alice's private office/bedroom was near the entry to the dorm and she kept the area neat, clean, and welcoming to the girls.

# SISTER MARY ALICE

I was getting to know Sister Mary Alice on a personal basis. She was very approachable, partly because she was short and not a threatening presence. When she saw me coming, I'm sure she had to brace herself, as she never knew what questions I had for her.

That year I had started to notice boys, and I had questions—questions that I couldn't even ask my mom.

During one visit to her office, I had questions about Sister Mary Alice herself, her life and where she'd come from. On this particular visit, I remember that I was curious about whether she had a family, brothers, sisters, parents. She seemed to drift off as she quietly described Quebec, the gardens, and herself as a young girl standing in the fields. Her words were filled with emotion, like good memories.

I asked her if she had ever had a boyfriend and then I followed up quickly with, "Are you a eunuch, you know, like, not human?"

She held back her immediate response, or I'm sure she would have burst out laughing. But I was quite serious, so she answered—with some restraint. She smiled, and, with a little chuckle, she said, "No!"

To this day, I don't know where the word "eunuch" came from. The word seemed to fit descriptions of people who had no gender, but it certainly was not in my mom's vocabulary. I felt relief that Sister Mary Alice was not a eunuch, and with that out of the way, I returned to my own matters.

# MORNINGS

The daily morning routine included Sister Mary Alice walking up and down the hallway, ringing a hand bell. It was as if the bell was begging us to please get out of bed. I had a hard time waking up every morning. My only thoughts were how much I wished I could just sleep.

There was a daily morning Mass that anyone could go to. We had to attend at least three daily masses for the week and, of course, the obligation of Sunday.

The chapel was located at the end part of an older building and the entrance was a single door with an entry area. Off to the left was the sacred room with a little font of holy water attached to the wall just inside the doorway. Everyone was welcome to bless themselves as they entered the chapel.

Wooden pews filled most of the room, and at the end was an altar. The Mass was celebrated in Latin, and all of the statues were there to witness the services. My memory was that it was usually Father J. Spils who led us in prayer, facing the altar and away from us. He was a quiet sort of man, very private, and generally kept to himself. He, too, was interesting to me, but I didn't dare speak to him about my crazy questions—after all, he was a man.

Breakfasts were fast and furious. Sister Mary Ida and her kitchen crew were always prepared to serve the hot meals that varied from morning to morning. The students formed a chow line, waiting until it was time to receive our food after taking metal, military style trays, silverware, cups, and plastic water glasses.

*Tiny at CVS high school.*

One favorite morning meal of mine was the corn bread breakfast. I never had corn bread before, but it was great. Each serving of the bread was huge. I'd quickly cut the bread and spread it with butter, and as the butter melted the corn bread was ready for the hot syrup. It was a meal all to itself.

After breakfast, some students had their chores to attend to, and some would go back to the dorm to get ready for the school day. I was now in the eighth grade, getting ready for high school.

*Teenage Tiny and a young cousin.*

# CVS GLEE CLUB, 1960 to 1961

The year I was 15, CVS had a Glee Club, and Miss Gen Hetu was our music teacher. Just a young woman herself, she loved her work and organized a girls' quartet, boys' quartet and, combining the two groups, an octet. Miss Gen worked us hard and her enthusiasm was contagious. She found new versions of old songs that sparked our energy and woke up our spirits, leaving us all with a new appreciation for the human voice.

That year, we sang our hearts out. It was the year that our

small Copper Valley High School went to the statewide competition in Fairbanks and competed against schools from Anchorage and Fairbanks, places where talent came from a large pool of students.

We arrived in our old rattling school bus, the girls' quartet wearing their school sweaters, white blouses, and red ribbons fashioned into ties. The boys were decked out with top hats and their school sweaters.

We sang the "Muskrat Rambler Song," "The Green Leaves of Summer," and other popular songs. We were animated and in great form. We stole the show, though, when we belted out the last verse of "I've Been Working on the Railroad!" and kicked it into a sexy, jazzy ending. I remember the reactions of several of the other schools' kids, wondering who we were and where had we come from. They loved us!

Unfortunately for us, the music director for a Fairbanks high school had us disqualified from the competition. The reason she claimed was that no one else had access to the music arrangements that Miss Gen had found for us, and therefore it was an unfair competition. But the "damage" was done, because we had already won the hearts of the other contestants. This was evident in their disappointed reaction when they heard the announcement of our disqualification.

Miss Gen took on the challenge of teaching us the complicated "Hallelujah Chorus" from Handel's *Messiah* for our Christmas pageant. She told us the song was so powerful that if we did a good job, the audience would not react right away—that there would be silence for a short period of time before the audience would applaud. I didn't quite understand in that moment what she was talking about.

Finally, after many days and long hours of practice, it was show time. People came for the Christmas pageant from all the surrounding communities—Glennallen, Copper Center, Gakona, and even Valdez. They joined the audience with our student body, volunteers, clergy, support staff, and teachers.

The "Hallelujah Chorus" was the last song of the evening.

When it was time for it, we knew it might be the last time we would sing it together, so we sang our hearts out. When it was over, it was as Miss Gen had predicted. The audience just sat there in silence for a few long seconds. Just as we were wondering what happened, people started cheering. Their reaction was astounding.

Miss Gen had tears rolling down her cheeks when she winked, smiled, and gave us a signal that it was perfect. Miss Gen had taken us high school kids and shaped us into an amazing choir.

# The SPIRIT of COPPER VALLEY

In the beginning, no one knew that CVS was to have a short window of existence, only fifteen years from 1956 to 1971.

Those of us who were either recruited, drawn to, or stumbled upon CVS shared the amazing experience of Copper Valley. We refer to it as the "Spirit of Copper Valley," cherish it and hold on to it as our sense of family.

My six years there were a source of strength, the beginning of long friendships, and spirit as a driving force of values to pass on to my son, daughter and grandson. The leadership that was developed there in us demonstrates that a Catholic boarding school, if done right, can build and sustain future generations.

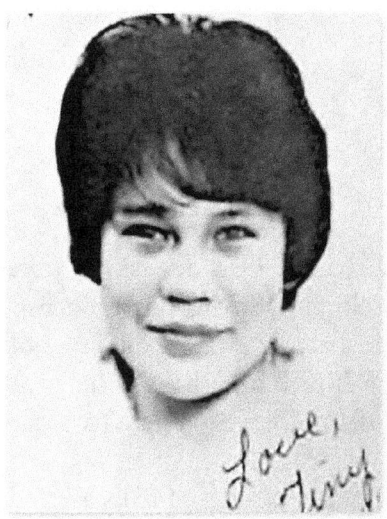

*Tiny Demientieff, Copper Valley School graduation photo.*

*Editor's Note:*

*Tiny's Stories culminate here with her high school experiences at Copper Valley School. Readers should note that in contrast to 20th century Native boarding school histories ranging from unpleasant to horrific, student testimonies collected from CVS are overall positive. CVS operated between 1956 and 1971, before state-required high schools were built in Alaska's Native villages. For families living in remote and roadless areas during this time, CVS provided one of very few opportunities for a high-quality secondary education. Towns and villages throughout Alaska were represented in the CVS student body, which was multi-racial and included many local students as well as foreign exchange students.*

# TINY'S EPILOGUE

*A Near-Death Experience*

One summer, while living in Fairbanks, Dad decided to take our family on a road trip to Circle Hot Springs. It took two cars to get us there, since we had friends along—a couple of boys who were good friends of Birdie and Bing. One was Red, a mischievous boy with red hair who liked to tease Sugar, Tootie, and me.

The ride was long, hot and dusty, and when we finally arrived at the resort, we hurried into our swimming suits and into the indoor pool. We were full of energy.

After all the teasing we'd had from Red, Sugar and Tootie and I decided to gang up on him and throw him into the deep end of the pool. It was a foolish idea, since Red was bigger and stronger than the three of us. He simply tossed me into the pool. We were at the deep end and I didn't know how to swim.

The water was warm. As I plunged down, I remember seeing all the bubbles. It was all so sudden that I didn't struggle, I just watched those bubbles. Then I was overcome by some very unusual music—relaxing, mystical, and inviting. The sounds were like soft chimes, and I saw rose colors all around. I started to float, drawn into a light in the distance. As I drifted, my feelings and thoughts melted away and I felt no emotion. As I was drawn closer to the light, I became more relaxed and blissful, as if the world was releasing me.

I was so joyous, and then just as I was about to reach that light, Lolly grabbed me by my hair and yanked me out of the water. I clearly recall I wanted to slap her, as I didn't want to let go of the moment or come back. All of a sudden, I was filled with anger, frustration, and confusion. I couldn't talk about it, or tell anyone. It was a memory I kept to myself.

Years later as an adult, I was at a conference in Tok and

during a lunch break a small group of participants started talking of their near-death experiences. I sat and listened and then, because I finally felt safe enough, I talked about my experience in the water.

We ended up comparing the different colors we'd each seen, none of us sure what they might mean. Many years later, I heard of others sharing their near-death stories, too. I still cherish the memory!

Thinking back, I believe that in the departure of worldly emotions, I was experiencing love and letting go. It was like the process of dying. After that experience, I have no fear of dying. The sadness of death for me is loss, loss of a loved one or a close friend, but for me, dying will be that same transition to love, and the light.

# MEMORIAL BIOGRAPHY OF THERESA "TINY" DEVLIN

*By Jack Devlin and Sam Demientieff*

*Theresa "Tiny" Devlin was born August 18, 1945, in Nenana, Alaska. She was the eighth of ten children of Nick and Nellie Demientieff. Tiny, as she was known to all, was a light-hearted, mischievous young person who grew into an independent, caring woman, for whom her Native culture, individual and community well-being were paramount.*

*Various Alaskan communities benefited from Tiny's outlook, advocacy, knowledge and love for Native life, embodying this love which has shaped communities in Alaska from our very beginnings* as a state.

*Tiny was a river Native, a Deg Xit'an Athabascan woman who grew up on her parents' barges that ran freight up and down the Yukon and Tanana Rivers. Her appreciation for humor, a genuine good story, and her fine memory for details of life and spirituality drove her to write stories documenting her life.*

*Tiny was dedicated to the love of her life, Jack Devlin, and they married on June 22, 1973. Tiny embraced his kids and always valued family and togetherness—they each and all were her kids, too. Together, Tiny and Jack raised Justin and Vincent, Scott, Eric, and their own and youngest child, Jacklynn Devlin. Tiny was a role model to them of strength and dignity—but always with heart and smiles. She often asked, "Are you happy?" She wanted her kids and those around her to live a good life and to do the right thing—and do it with a real taste for life.*

*Tiny showed great courage to her family with pulmonary fibrosis, not disclosing all the challenges or natural fears it may have engendered. She did not want people to fear for her. To the very end, many were witness to her strength and courage and how she bravely crossed over.*

*Tiny went to grade school in Fairbanks, high school at Copper Valley. At CVS, she was a cheerleader and served on the student body council. She graduated there. As an adult, she later served on the board of directors for the Copper Valley Alumni Association.*

*Some of Tiny's interesting life experiences as an adult include working as an LPN at the Alaska Psychiatric Institute (API). It is a little-known fact that Tiny was a champion junior dog sled racer, and traveled widely as a traveling spiritual healer.*

*Her love of a good story made her well suited for her job as a director and producer at KAKM, Channel 7 Public Television in Anchorage. She inspired many, sharing personal strengths and those found in one's culture. She inspired many others when she served as a University of Alaska Fairbanks Leadership Coordinator, organizing opportunities for emerging leaders with cultural experiences in Australia, New Zealand, and in the Amazon among the Yanomami people of the rainforest. She served on an advisory committee for the University of Washington. She also worked in the Enrollment Division of the historic Alaska Native Claims Settlement Act. At another time, she was employed by the Anchorage Diocese of the Catholic Church in the area of advocacy.*

*Tiny participated in the Gathering of Native Americans, a decades-old proven model for healing, in the capacity of building wellness in Native villages and communities.*

*To the very last day of her life, Tiny promoted wellness and spirituality and happiness in her family and among her friends. She impacted all those who came near her with her love of life, cultural foods, and with her penchant for story and laughter. Tiny loved her Holy Cross King salmon strips, banana nut bread, and spicy Russian tea.*

*Tiny believed in Native people authoring their own wellness and history, and the life where they lived. She was an eloquent advocate of the Native experience and also the responsibility of all people to come to terms with their personal and collective histories. She didn't shy away from holding strong opinions, favoring what was best for truth-telling, healing, and giving voice to those that might be otherwise marginalized. She was an extraordinary figure in our time. Her life inspired many, and will continue to inspire many yet.*

*Tiny wrote articles-memories of her childhood growing up on Alaskan rivers for the* Tundra Times *and was in the process of writing this book at the end of her life.*

# TINY AND JACK DEVLIN

*Tiny and Jack with young family. Left to right: Vince, Scott, Justin, Tiny, Eric, Jacklynn, and Jack.*

# *ACKNOWLEDGMENTS*

Assisting Jack Devlin and Tiny and Jack's daughter, Jacklynn, in the creation of this book were Sam Demientieff, Tiny's older brother, and his wife, Mary Demientieff. Sam provided map information plus narratives of historical background and the family's river barge company, Demientieff Navigation. Sam and Mary were able to fill in important details and background for *Tiny's Stories* and brought many photos from their collection to illustrate the book.

Mickey (Grinzell) King, a retired archivist for the Sisters of Saint Ann, was a friend of Tiny's and a fellow student at Copper Valley School. Mickey contributed valuable research and background for this book all through the long process of bringing it to print.

Tiny's friend and fellow KAKM producer, Carroll Hodge, worked with Tiny as these stories were written, offering encouragement and friendship, as well as giving a first form to the stories and composing the book's Foreword. She provided editing and important insights throughout the book-making process.

Stephen (Guy) Gemmell of the Copper Valley School Alumni Association contributed photos and information from the school and its newsletters. During the writing of her stories, Tiny had corresponded with many of her fellow CVS alumni about their school days and the planned book. Thanks go out to all of these friends of Tiny for their encouragement and support. Thank you to Mariah Pitka for making early copies of the book for family and friends.

Thanks also to Irene Rowan, who assured Tiny that her stories would find a home in print. Irene continued that assurance with ideas and kind comments for the book as we prepared the book for publication. Early on, Irene pointed Tiny's family to Lisa Alexia of Denali Sunrise Publications. Lisa, in turn, pointed Jack and Jacklynn toward Mary Odden for work on the manuscript. Lisa, a fount of book know-how, stayed with the project on the sidelines and gave important advice. Mary edited the manuscript for publication, folded in details from family and friends and beyond. Kari Odden of Moontide Design worked with photos, created maps with Sam, designed the cover and text for review copies. Throughout all of this process, the circle of family and friends of *Tiny's Stories* kept growing – a whole village to raise a book.

## *About Cirque Press*

Cirque Press grew out of *Cirque*, a literary journal that publishes the works of writers and artists from the North Pacific Rim, a region that reaches north from Oregon to the Yukon Territory, south through Alaska to Hawaii, and west to the Russian Far East.

Cirque Press is a partnership of Sandra Kleven, publisher, and Michael Burwell, editor. Ten years ago, we recognized that works of talented writers in the region were going unpublished, and the Press was launched to bring those works to fruition. We publish fiction, nonfiction, and poetry, and we seek to produce art that provides a deeper understanding about the region and its cultures. The writing of our authors is significant, personal, and strong.

Sandra Kleven – Michael Burwell, publishers and editors
www.cirquejournal.com

# BOOKS *from Cirque Press*

*Apportioning the Light* by Karen Tschannen (2018)

*The Lure of Impermanence* by Carey Taylor (2018)

*Echolocation* by Kristin Berger (2018)

*Like Painted Kites & Collected Works* by Clifton Bates (2019)

*Athabaskan Fractal: Poems of the Far North* by Karla Linn Merrifield (2019)

*Holy Ghost Town* by Tim Sherry (2019)

*Drunk on Love: Twelve Stories to Savor Responsibly* by Kerry Dean Feldman (2019)

*Wide Open Eyes: Surfacing from Vietnam* by Paul Kirk Haeder (2020)

*Silty Water People* by Vivian Faith Prescott (2020)

*Life Revised* by Leah Stenson (2020)

*Oasis Earth: Planet in Peril* by Rick Steiner (2020)

*The Way to Gaamaak Cove* by Doug Pope (2020)

*Loggers Don't Make Love* by Dave Rowan (2020)

*The Dream That Is Childhood* by Sandra Wassilie (2020)

*Seward Soundboard* by Sean Ulman (2020)

*The Fox Boy* by Gretchen Brinck (2021)

*Lily Is Leaving: Poems* by Leslie Ann Fried (2021)

*One Headlight* by Matt Caprioli (2021)

*November Reconsidered* by Marc Janssen (2021)

*Callie Comes of Age* by Dale Champlin (2021)

*Someday I'll Miss This Place Too* by Dan Branch (2021)

*Out There In The Out There* by Jerry McDonnell (2021)

*Fish the Dead Water Hard* by Eric Heyne (2021)

*Salt & Roses* by Buffy McKay (2022)

*Growing Older In This Place: A Life in Alaska's Rainforest* by Margo Wasserman Waring (2022)

*Kettle Dance: A Big Sky Murder* by Kerry Dean Feldman (2022)

*Nothing Got Broke* by Larry F. Slonaker (2022)

*On the Beach: Poems 2016-2021* by Alan Weltzien (2022)

*Sky Changes on the Kuskokwim* by Clifton Bates (2022)

*Transplanted* by Birgit Lennertz Sarrimanolis (2022)

*Between Promise and Sadness* by Joanne Townsend (2022)

*Yosemite Dawning* by Shauna Potocky (2022)

*The Woman Within* by Tami Phelps and Kerry Dean Feldman (2023)

*In the Winter of the Orange Snow* by Diane S. Carpenter (2023)

*Mail Order Nurse* by Sue Lium (2023)

*All in Due Time* by Kate Troll (2023)

*Infinite Meditations For Inspiration and Daily Practice* by Scott Hanson (2023)

*Getting Home from Here* by Anne Ward-Masterson (2023)

*Crossing the Burnside Bridge & Other Poems* by Janice D. Rubin (2023)

*May the Owl Call Again: A Return to Poet John Meade Haines, 1924–2011* by Rachel Epstein (2023)

## CIRCLES *Illustrated books from Cirque Press*

*Baby Abe: A Lullaby for Lincoln* by Ann Chandonnet (2021)

*Miss Tami, Is Today Tomorrow?* by Tami Phelps (2021)

*Miss Bebe Goes to America* by Lynda Humphrey (2022)

MORE PRAISE FOR

## *TINY'S STORIES: AN ATHABASCAN FAMILY ON THE YUKON RIVER*

Tiny's book is a breath of fresh air, sharing her unique life on her father's river boat. Her book describes the strength and importance of her close-knit family, Athabascan values passed down from both her parents. She tells her story as though she is having an intimate conversation with the reader. As she grows older, she questions the meaning of her life, nurtures her spirituality, and always maintains her sense of humor and zest for life, integral parts of her character and personality. They carried her through her own challenges. The world needs positive people like Tiny who add joy and laughter to our lives. Her book accomplishes that and is also a vivid and delightful slice of one family's history on the river.

—Eileen Norbert, author of *Menadelook: An Inupiat Teacher's Photographs of Alaska Village Life, 1907–1932*

Rather than working for wages, Tiny's parents risked starting their own business to supplement their traditional subsistence lifestyle. The family living and working together on the boats from May through September made a strong team. Reading the stories, I was transported back to my early years in the mining town of Ruby on the Yukon River. Tiny's stories of 60 and 70 years ago also point out the sharp ecological contrast with today. Because of climate change, with warmer temperatures and loss of permafrost, the rivers are not safe to travel in winter and many lakes are meadows now. The fish camps are gone because there are no salmon. People cannot live out on the land in the same way they did when Nick and Nellie Demientieff's family was young.

—Walter (Wally) Carlo, Fairbanks

I was blessed to be one of Tiny's friends. Tiny had a lot of friends all over the world, and if she didn't know them, they surely knew her. She had an important voice, always, from her young days at Copper Valley School when I first knew her, all the way to Washington, DC where she spoke up for Indigenous people and health care. People counted on her measured opinions, and they listened to her. She had the precious gift of telling stories, from growing up with people who celebrate their history through stories. I can hear her spoken voice in these written stories. I laugh when I hear about Mrs. Anthony and the nuns, and I hear Tiny's pride and respect in the stories about her parents, her brothers and sisters. The reader will hear these things too.

> —Mickey Grinzell King, Archivist (ret.) Sisters
> of Saint Ann Archives, Victoria, BC

These stories draw an intimate portrait of an amazing family, nurtured in the love of parents who gave them a firm grounding. Drawn immediately to the riverboat stories, I was soon also struck by the wide exposure Tiny and the other children gained in different aspects of post-WW II Alaska. Tiny's brother, Sam, talked about how the freighting life fostered friendships all along the rivers, friendships that became important when he later served in many important positions in the state. Finally, Tiny's vignettes from the Copper Valley School, where she and several siblings attended, are a window into Native schooling that will take readers beyond simple good or bad characterizations of the religious boarding schools.

> —William Schneider, Professor Emeritus, Alaska
> and Polar Regions - UAF Rasmuson Library

Tiny is my 2nd cousin on my mother's side, but I first met her when I went to school at CVS. I was best friends with her sister Irene. In the summer they all lived on a freight boat, traveling the Mighty Yukon. I believe her life on the river, her family, and her school experiences all helped her be so at ease with so many people. Tiny had humor, wit, and the joy of life. We never lost touch, and later in life Tiny shared some of the stories she was working on with me. I loved the humor in them. Like her father and her brother Sam, she was a great storyteller.

> —Patty Baldwin, McGrath and Fairbanks

www.ingramcontent.com/pod-product-compliance
Lightning Source LLC
LaVergne TN
LVHW010333070526
838199LV00065B/5738